POST-
ABORTION
TRAUMA

POST-ABORTION TRAUMA

9 Steps to Recovery

Jeanette Vought

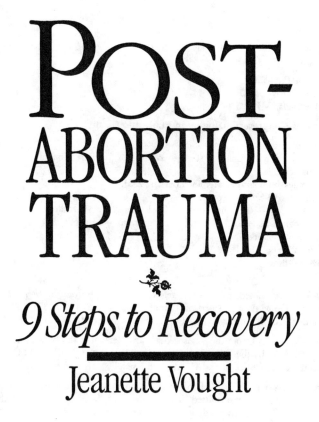

ZondervanPublishingHouse
Grand Rapids, Michigan

A Division of HarperCollins*Publishers*

POST-ABORTION TRAUMA: 9 STEPS TO RECOVERY
COPYRIGHT © 1991 JEANETTE VOUGHT

Zondervan Publishing House
1415 Lake Drive, S.E.
Grand Rapids, MI 49506

Library of Congress Cataloging-in-Publication Data

Vought, Jeanette.
     Post-abortion trauma : 9 steps to recovery / Jeanette Vought.
         p. cm.
     Includes bibliographical references (p. 255).
     ISBN 0-310-53641-3 (paper)
     1. Abortion—Religious aspects—Christianity. 2. Abortion—
Psychological aspects. 3. Twelve-step programs—Religious aspects—
Christianity. I. Title.
HQ767.25.V68   1991
363.4'6—dc20   91–13443
                                                                          CIP

Unless otherwise noted, all Scripture references are taken from the *Holy Bible: New International Version* (North American Edition), copyright © 1973, 1978, 1984 by the International Bible Society. Used by permission of Zondervan Bible Publishers.

Scripture quotations from the Revised Standard Version of the Bible are copyright 1946, 1952, 1971 by the Division of Christian Education of the National Council of the Churches of Christ in the U.S.A. and used by permission.

Edited by Linda Vanderzalm
Interior Design by Kim Koning
Cover Design and Photo by Gary Gnidovic

Printed in the United States of America

91   92   93   94   95 / AK / 10   9   8   7   6   5   4   3   2   1

I dedicate this book to the women and men who have told their stories here so that other women and men may be helped. Their courage and determination to work toward recovery has been an encouragement and incentive for me to write this book.

Contents

Acknowledgments

I wish to thank the many people who have given invaluable support to this project, both in their involvement with the Conquerors post-abortion recovery program, the development and implementation of the Conquerors survey, and the preparation of materials.

For their help in developing the Conquerors program manual, including the nine steps to recovery, I'm sincerely grateful to:

> Janna Poage, former director, Conquerors in Minneapolis;
>
> Judy Anderson, coordinator, Conquerors North;
>
> Marlene Schuler, former director, Conquerors in Rochester, Minnesota;
>
> Julie Gehrke, former director, Conquerors in Minneapolis/St. Paul;
>
> Rebecca Holmlund, former coordinator, Conquerors in Minneapolis.

The introductory material, the nine steps, the forms, and the homework questions from Part III of this book are derived from the Conquerors manual, to which each of these women has contributed. The manual, which describes in greater detail how to conduct Conquerors post-abortion support groups, can be purchased from:

New Life Family Services
1515 E. 66th St.
Richfield, MN 55423

I also thank the staff at New Life Family Services ministry of the Greater Minnesota Association of Evangelicals for their encouragement and support for this project.

I give special thanks to Dr. Ruth Bolton (Unit Director of the North Memorial Family Practice Residency; Assistant Professor at the University of Minnesota, Department of Family Practice and Community Health) for sharing her expertise about the physical aspects of abortion in chapter 6. Ruth's dedication to the sanctity of the human life is evident to all who work with her.

I'm very grateful to Joyce Ellis for her countless hours typing, editing, and bringing this book to completion. Without her support and exceptional writing gifts, this book would not have been written. Joyce also suggested additional resource materials and Scripture verses that added to the content of the book.

Finally, I'm deeply thankful for my dear husband, Ron Vought, who gave me the encouragement and freedom to write this book. Even though it took countless hours of my family time, he unselfishly supported this venture at his own expense and comfort. I'm also thankful for the faithful support I received from our four sons—Daniel, Jonathan, Michael, and Matthew—and their wives—Lori, Shirley, and Therese.

The ultimate thanks and praise belong to God, who gave me the vision, strength, and wisdom to write this book. He was always with me, guiding and directing in the way that I should go.

Introduction

National statistics indicate that since the Supreme Court's *Roe* v. *Wade* decision in 1973, over 25 million abortions have been reported in the United States. And the 25 million unborn children were not the only victims of these abortions. Somewhere, for every aborted baby, lives a woman and man who were responsible for that baby's conception— and abortion. Many of those women and men struggle for years in the aftermath of the abortion, living with guilt, anger, shame, and confusion.

This book describes the trauma women and men experience after aborting their babies. Both women and men openly share their experiences, hoping that in telling their stories, they will help someone else through the anguish of a post-abortion experience.

Part I will help readers understand the complexity of the abortion problem: its scope, the church's response, and its sources. Part II will help readers understand who is affected by abortion (from the unborn child and its parents to the abortionists) as well as how they are affected physically, emotionally, and spiritually. Part III describes the history of the Conquerors post-abortion support program (begun by New Life Family Services, a ministry of the Greater Minnesota Association of Evangelicals) and the importance of Conquerors men's post-abortion support groups. Part IV outlines a nine-step recovery program designed by Conquerors.

The nine-step recovery program helps post-abortive women and men find healing and personal growth through small support groups that explore the dynamics of the post-abortion experience from a biblical perspective. This section of the book includes detailed chapters about facing the realities of the abortion experience; dealing with the powerful feelings of anxiety, fear, shame, guilt, and grief; forgiving oneself and others involved in the abortion; and developing a positive self-image. Each chapter includes relevant Scripture passages as well as study questions that will help post-abortive women and men work toward healing.

I hope that this book will help not only the women and men who have gone through an abortion experience but also the people who try to help them through this experience—family members, friends, medical personnel, pastors, and counselors. For too long the Christian church has ignored the problems post-abortive women and men face. It is time for the body of Christ to be a prophetic voice, calling people to righteous living and obedience to God's design for his people. It is time for the body of Christ to be an informed healing agent that will bring hope, forgiveness, and peace to women and men whose lives have been shattered by post-abortion trauma.

PART I

Understanding the Problem

1

How Did We Get into This Mess?

Cara's (not her real name) mother wasn't married when she became pregnant with Cara, and her only advice to her daughter about sex was, "I hope you wait until you're at least seventeen, and don't do it with anyone unless you love him enough to marry him."

Tormented by the cruelty of peers who called her names like Big Nose and Crater Face, Cara's self-esteem lay in tatters. She tried to overcome this rejection in her early teen years through involvement in sports and cheerleading. "I thought that if I could prove to them that I was good at these things," she says, "then they would want to be my friends and I would become popular." But Cara soon realized that no matter how involved she became, the popular crowd would never accept her. She didn't meet the requirements for acceptance: a pretty face and a vivacious, often false, personality.

When she was fifteen, Cara met a handsome, seventeen-year-old Middle Eastern young man. "He adored me," she says, "and made me feel more loved than anyone ever had.

Every feature I didn't like about myself, he loved. He worshiped me, and I was amazed." Cara became sexually involved with the boy, rationalizing, "I love him, and why should I wait until I'm seventeen? I already know it all."

While she was a student at a Christian high school the following year, Cara saw her need to repent. She gave her sins to God and accepted Christ as her Savior, not yet fully understanding all that meant.

A new Christian and still sexually active, Cara spent the rest of the year trying to get her Muslim boyfriend to surrender his life to Christ. When he didn't respond, she tried repeatedly to break off the relationship, but it was too hard. By January of her senior year, Cara was pregnant. "Although I hadn't done anything to prevent this from happening, it was still a shock," she says. "I was happy and terrified at the same time."

Having finally found acceptance at the Christian school, Cara dreaded the disgrace of facing her teachers and classmates, and she hated letting down her parents. "I had led them to believe I was a 'good girl,'" she says. Cara couldn't tell her mother. She tried, but all she could do was cry. Her mother guessed the problem. After several days of Cara's hysterical sobbing, her parents (not particularly religious people) and her boyfriend's guardians decided that abortion was the only solution.

Cara resisted. She believed that abortion was murder. But when she realized that she wasn't going to get any practical help from anyone in raising the baby, she began to consider the option. "I toyed with the idea of telling the one adult I trusted most at my Christian school, but the risk seemed too great," she remembers. "What if she had no answers either? What if she couldn't help? Then my secret would be out, and I wouldn't have a chance of handling the situation without anyone knowing. The secrecy, shame, guilt, and desperation took their toll. I emptied myself of all emotion and spirituality and agreed to have an abortion. I felt I had no choice. My parents wanted me to have a good life, a college education, and the freedom to achieve all my dreams. I think they also feared their inability to weather this unbearable crisis."

Cara was nine weeks pregnant when she had the abortion. "As I left the clinic, I felt sure that hell would open up and swallow me," she says.

Cara's story is not an isolated one, yet too long we have denied that Christian women have abortions. Now more and more women are breaking the silence and looking to the church for help. What causes a woman to seek an abortion? How does abortion affect the woman and those around her? And how can the Christian church help women with crisis pregnancies?

SOCIETY'S ATTITUDES TOWARD SEXUALITY AND CRISIS PREGNANCY

Have we outgrown the 1960s "me-generation" attitudes or do they still permeate the 1990s? Our society tells us that a person's individual rights are most important. We should be able to enjoy pleasure and self-fulfillment regardless of how our actions affect ourselves and others. And if something is inconvenient or gets in the way of our goals or pleasures, we have the right to get rid of it.

We especially see these attitudes in the areas of sex, unwanted pregnancies, and abortions. More and more people live by the standard "if it feels good do it."

As *Time* magazine verifies, virginity is not popular. "A 1982 survey conducted by Johns Hopkins researchers John

Kantner and Melvin Zelnick found that nearly one out of five 15-year-old girls admitted that they had already had intercourse, as did nearly a third of 16-year-olds and 43% of 17-year-olds. 'In the eyes of their peers, it is important for kids to be sexually active. No one wants to be a virgin,' observes Amy Williams, director of San Francisco's Teenage Pregnancy and Parenting Project (TAPP).'[1]

If a woman becomes pregnant and the baby is an inconvenience or embarrassment, society's answer is abortion. Women and men caught in crisis pregnancies are easy prey. In desperation they look for someone to give them an answer. When abortion is described as "disposing of unwanted tissue mass," it sounds like an appealing, easy solution.

One young woman who called a crisis pregnancy center where I worked desperately wanted some answers but wasn't getting the help she needed from an abortion clinic. When she called me, she wanted advice because she couldn't follow through on the abortion appointments she had made. When I asked her how many appointments she had made, she told me she had made seventeen. I could hardly believe it. I wondered why the abortion clinic kept rescheduling appointments when she obviously wasn't sure she wanted to have the procedure.

Media Messages

The media also give messages that lead women and men to choose abortion. Youth worker Jerry Johnston, in his book *Going All The Way*, talks about the real world of sex and teens. Recapping some of his concerns, Johnston states, "This overall lowering of public values has contributed significantly to the rising sexual crises occurring in our country. What caused such a lowering of our nation's moral conscience? . . . It was the acceptance of a philosophy of accommodation . . . giving the OK to any and all types of sexual practice."[2]

Johnston further states that this philosophy of accommodation is *encouraged* by the media:

> [Music]: The medium of entertainment shouts out a philosophy of sex outside of marriage, of sex outside of commitment, of sex outside of reason. . . .

> [Television]: From the free love portrayed in TV soap operas, to TV talk shows, to prime-time television shows . . . showing little sexual restraint . . . television proclaims that sexual freedom is good, normal and to be encouraged. . . .

> [Publications]: From *Playboy* to *Cosmopolitan,* magazines glorify marital infidelity and premarital sex.[3]

Of course, this influence has spread much further. Sensuality seems to be the key word in advertising today. Semi-nudity is common.

Educational Messages

Sexual freedom and abortion messages have also invaded our educational system. Jerry Johnston says,

> In growing numbers public schools are dispensing condoms to teens, without parental knowledge or consent. We must do it, administrators have told me. Why? Because teenagers are going to be sexually active anyway, so let's make it safe for them. This is in place of any teaching of abstinence or other moral instruction.

> This pervasive attitude of accommodating any sexual activity is forcing us now to accommodate the risk of teen pregnancy, AIDS and STDs [sexually transmitted diseases]. Many kids have asked me if anything can really be called "wrong" anymore.[4]

Although today's society sees teen pregnancy as a problem, it advocates sex education, contraceptives, and abortion as the solution. Instead of preventing pregnancies, however, these methods may have contributed to an increase in teen pregnancies. According to the National Center for Health Statistics, in 1985, the number of pregnancies among unmarried girls between the ages fifteen to nineteen was 270,922, while the number of pregnancies of those younger than fifteen was 9,386.[5]

It appears that the message our young people are receiving is that it's okay to be sexually active before marriage and that contraceptives are the means to preventing unwanted pregnancies. Anytime adults seem to condone the use of contraceptives without emphasizing sexual abstinence, our young people may assume that adults approve of their sexual activity.

Parental Messages

Society's attitude toward sexual behavior and crisis pregnancies are also expressed in the family. Parents send several kinds of messages.

Many parents find it difficult to talk directly about sex with their children. Instead, they send indirect messages of fear, suspicion, or disapproval, hoping their children will avoid sexual activity. Sometimes these parental attitudes actually encourage sexual experimentation. The kids reason that if their parents think they're doing it anyway, they might as well go ahead and do it.

The family atmosphere the parents set also affects their children's sexual behavior. If parents create a nurturing environment for their children, the children will feel loved and accepted. If young people feel that their parents listen to them and understand them, they will feel more free to discuss their sexuality. If kids do not receive this acceptance and nurturing within the family setting, they may go outside the family to their peer group, which often has a different value system. Many young people who become sexually active don't want to be, but they need someone to love them, to listen to them, and to understand them.

Some parents lay down no boundaries for their children and allow them to do whatever they want. Without the security of boundaries, children can feel confused. In their attempt to find standards, they look to peers, the media, or other adults, who may not be positive role models for them.

Other parents set unreasonably harsh standards, leaving children feeling angry, disillusioned, and hopeless. In Ephesians 6:4, the apostle Paul warns fathers (parents), "Do not exasperate your children; instead, bring them up in the training and instruction of the Lord." If parental standards, however biblical, become too rigid, children don't see the love behind the standards.

Parents send another message when they encourage children to grow up too fast—allowing early dating, use of heavy makeup, or seductive clothing. Many parents unintentionally try to boost their own self-esteem by promoting their children. If their daughter (as young as ten or eleven) looks just the right way or attracts the right boy, the parents can see some of their own unfulfilled dreams come true.

THE ABORTION CRISIS

Our young people have paid a high price in buying the messages that society has been peddling. In recent years the teen pregnancy rate has been increasing, and—here lies the crisis—forty-five percent of all pregnant teens in the U.S. have abortions. That's almost one out of two. Thirty percent of all abortions in the United States are performed on teenagers. And these young women are not all from poor families. Many of them come from middle- to upper-income families.[6] Our culture has closed its eyes to the pain young people and their families experience from society's solutions to sexuality, crisis pregnancies, and abortion.

Our society has tried to convince us that abortion gives women more freedom, but many women who have had an abortion find themselves anything but free—from guilt, shame, anger, grief, loss of self-esteem, and feelings of exploitation. Instead of selling women a Bill of Rights, perhaps our society has sold them a bill of goods.

A Woman's Right to Choose

Society has promoted the right of the woman to choose an abortion for her child, regardless of the reason. Unfortunately, society does not recognize the woman's right to know what her other choices are.

Society ignores her right to know the physical, emotional, and spiritual complications she may suffer from having an abortion. If a woman knew that she may struggle with a sense of loss, guilt, and grief for years after the abortion experience, would she still have an abortion?

Society ignores her right to have information about fetal development. If a woman could see ultrasound pictures of her live, well-developed baby at eight weeks, would she still have an abortion?

Society ignores her right to take time to weigh the options and make the best decision for her baby and herself. If a woman wasn't pressured into a decision and could consult with family or people who could help her make an informed decision, would she still have an abortion? The middle of a crisis is not the time to make important decisions without counsel. Women facing crisis pregnancies are very vulnerable.

While society believes it is providing women with the freedom of choice, it is instead exploiting them, sentencing them to bondage. Society's highest goal seems to be that a woman rid herself of any inconvenience, no matter what the consequences are to the babies, women, fathers, and parents.

Parents Sometimes Have No Rights

Society also denies several basic rights to other people involved in the abortion experience. In many states, a minor child is able to have an abortion without her parents' consent. This same minor would not be allowed to have any other surgical procedure without parental consent. At a time when a young, pregnant daughter needs a great deal of support and counsel, her parents have no rights to know about the abortion or to have any say in whether or not their daughter has an abortion.

Pregnant Minors Sometimes Have No Rights

Or sometimes it is the pregnant woman herself who appears to have no rights. If a minor child doesn't want to abort her baby, sometimes the choice is made for her by the parents.

Dawn's Story

"When I was sixteen, I developed a relationship to the neighbor boy, Josh. This became a sexual relationship and continued until I was eighteen. I struggled to maintain as normal a personal life as possible in spite of the fact that my home life was so chaotic.

"In March 1976, I woke up very sick to my stomach. I

thought it was the flu, but every morning I continued to get sick. Finally realizing that I must be pregnant, I told Josh that if he would get a job, we could get married and have this baby. Josh thought this would be a good idea because we both would be graduating from high school in June.

"Not knowing how to approach the subject, after dinner one night I swallowed hard and blurted out, 'I'm pregnant.' My parents just about fell over.

"My father reacted by closing the drapes, locking the doors, and telling me to stay in *or else*. He was a leader in the church and community, and he was worried about his reputation. The next day my parents called a doctor and scheduled my abortion. They didn't ask me what I wanted to do with the baby; they were concerned only for themselves. Afraid of my father's often violent behavior, I stayed in the house as I was told.

"As I lay on a cot waiting to be called, I thought to myself, *What am I doing here?* I knew I didn't have a choice, though.

"When the doctor walked into the room to perform the abortion, he had blood all over his coat. I was so frightened that I nearly blocked everything else out. Intense pain shot through me as they clamped my uterus and used a vacuum tube to suck the baby from my body. Sorrow overwhelmed me. All at once, the atrocity of what I was doing hit me; *I was killing my baby!* It was too late to reverse the process. As they ripped my baby from me, I felt they were ripping my heart out too.

"When my mother took me home, she pretended nothing had happened.

"Shortly after the abortion, my father began beating me. One night he beat me so severely that I left the house and never went back. Shortly after graduation, I moved out of state.

"Even though I had left the negative home life of my family, my promiscuous behavior continued. I found a new boyfriend, with whom I immediately became sexually active. Again I became pregnant. The father of my baby had so many plans for his life that the thought of fathering a child seemed overwhelming. While I was excited about being pregnant, even wearing maternity clothes, he wanted me to get an abortion. I was devastated. But ultimately, wanting to please him, I agreed.

"The morning I arrived at the clinic for my second abortion, it was so crowded that I could find no place to sit.

"The experience was much the same as my first abortion, except that the staff treated me more like a number. I felt so stupid for having to go through an abortion a second time.

"In the recovery room a wall poster advertised women's rights. It said, 'If it weren't for us, where would you be today?' I hated that poster. I knew I'd be much happier without this 'right,' this right to kill.

"After my second abortion, I rationalized my decision to the point that I even began helping other women obtain abortions. Confused, I thought the feelings I had were over, but I was only repressing them.

"I took a job at an abortion clinic and began counseling women to have abortions. I told women that abortion was an easy, twenty-minute procedure. I felt so cool, so liberated.

"A year later reality hit once again. I began to feel very guilty about my own abortions and my counsel to others. I didn't know what to do with all the guilt and shame.

"God knew my turmoil and sent someone to tell me I didn't have to live with this guilt any longer. If I would ask

God to forgive me, I would be released from my guilt and shame.

"As I get to know Christ better and experience *his* love and forgiveness, I find it easier to forgive myself."

Dawn's story is similar to that of many other women who have struggled with crisis pregnancies resulting in abortions. Dawn was repeatedly victimized by the deeds of others and by society's freedom-to-choose messages. After thirteen years, she is beginning to experience freedom from the bondage of her past.

But women are not the only ones traumatized by abortions. The father of the aborted baby often feels an unbearable amount of pain.

Fathers Have No Rights

Fathers of aborted babies also have been denied rights. If a married woman wants to have an abortion, she can get one without the consent of her husband, the baby's father. A father is expected to support any child he helps conceive, yet he has no rights to stop the abortion process if he disagrees with his wife's decision

Gary's story gives us a glimpse of the pain and agony these men have felt after their abortion experiences.

Gary's Story

"It was the summer of 1981, a summer I'll never forget. I came home from work a little early to find my wife in tears. With fear and concern, I rushed to see what was wrong. After about ten minutes she was able to speak. What she had to say was something I didn't want to hear and something I couldn't comprehend. She told me she had had an abortion.

"I was shocked. I hadn't even known she had been pregnant. I felt used, unimportant, and so very alone. I grieved for the loss of my child. Nevertheless, I loved my wife and knew she needed me, so I tried to comfort her. At the same time I hurt inside like never before, and after I was alone, I cried for hours.

"A year after her abortion, my wife became pregnant again. This time she told me about it and I was pleased— until she told me she was going to have yet another abortion.

"I begged her not to do it. I told her I would be fully responsible for my child. I told her I would be willing to give the child up for adoption . . . just please don't kill my baby. She just turned and said, 'There's nothing you can do about it.'

"It would be impossible to describe the feelings I have. The emptiness, depression, and heartache are sometimes more than I can bear. I can use words like *pain* and *agony*, but these words just don't come close to telling the story as it really is.

I was having nightmares about the abortion, reliving the torment of that terrible day every time I went to sleep, waking up every night, feeling more depressed, hurting more each day. I still wanted to forget, but I began to realize that the feelings I had were not going to go away. I told myself I would have to live my pain in silence.

"Then it happened. She had the second abortion. With this abortion I felt more responsible because I had failed in my desperate attempt to save my child's life. I felt guilty and ashamed. I felt as if I had failed as a father for not being able to protect my child. I knew with all my heart that what my wife had done was wrong. And I prayed to God to please stop the torment and let me forget. I prayed to God to forgive me and my wife for what she had done. I knew that someone had to do something. But who? And what could they do? I felt alone and helpless.

"The abortions started to have a more noticeable effect on other areas of my life. They affected my performance on the job, my relationship to my friends, and the way I felt about myself. The abortions also have had an adverse effect on my health. I have developed two stress-related conditions.

"Then, in 1985, my wife became pregnant again. Her first thoughts again turned to abortion, but after three days of constant protest, I was able to talk her out of an abortion. We had a son. With the birth of our son came a new hope, and everything was okay. Or was it? I wanted my wife to be happy. I wanted my wife to enjoy our new son, and I wanted to be happy.

"The bonding between my son and me was incredible. I almost never left his side. I was there for his every need. I never even let him cry. I spoiled the kid rotten.

"When he would sleep, I monitored his breathing. I couldn't take anything for granted because I had already lost two children. And this little kid was here, and I was going to keep him. I had to be sure he was safe. I changed jobs, working nights so I could stay home days to take care of my son.

"After a while he began to trust only me. Sometimes he refused to eat unless I fed him. When he grew older, he would eat only whatever I had on my plate. Many times he would refuse to go to sleep unless I was the one who put him to bed.

"Even though my heart was filled with love for my wife and my son, it was also filled with a lot of hurt and pain. I'm sure my wife could see it in my eyes and hear it in my voice. We were truly trying to be happy, but it wasn't working. Finally after she began to hurt as I did for so many years, she asked for and received a divorce.

"The abortions have cost me my marriage, the lives of two of my children and after fourteen months of intense court battle, the custody of my three-year-old son, which is very difficult to accept.

"I know that many men are afraid to speak out because we've been told we have to hold our feelings in. We can't cry in public because we're men, we're strong. This is, in fact, what we *must* do. We *must* cry, we *must* share, we *must* open up and let someone know we are hurting. I want men to know and understand, if you refuse to share, if you refuse to cry, the pain you hold inside will destroy you. Please don't listen to those who tell you to take it like a man, because there is no way they can understand the pain and hurt, the emptiness and nightmares that you endure.

I want men and women who haven't been through this death experience to know and understand that our children constitute the greatest resource this country has. Our children hold the key to our future. Indeed they are our future. So let's hold them and feed them. Let's love them and clothe them. Let's educate them. Let's encourage their dreams and cherish their smiles as we watch them grow. And for God's sake, let's stop killing them."

2

Where Has the Church Been?

While society has been peddling its "freedom-to-choose" messages, where has the church been? How has it responded to sexuality, crisis pregnancy, and abortion among members of its congregations?

THE CHURCH'S RESPONSE

One young woman who has had an abortion says, "I'm angry that the church avoids dealing with the subject of sexuality. Why aren't there support groups for singles with sexual pressures? Support for girls who are pregnant? How about our Christian colleges? They barely admit there is even such a thing as sex, let alone create a safe place for women or men to go if they are treading in deep water. I wonder how many women get pregnant, have an abortion, and then go back to their colleges without telling anyone? When you're walking through hell in crisis, why isn't the church or Christian school a safe, unconditional loving place?"

Another young woman shares the havoc of living with shame and not feeling that she could go to her church to find answers. "My church was very legalistic, always preaching judgment. After I had become pregnant, I was afraid to talk with my pastor or church friends because I was sure they would preach at me and push me away for what I had done. I didn't feel as if I could talk to my parents either. We never talked about real things, and my parents always had a 'shaming' Bible verse for every situation. After I had an abortion, I felt even worse. But I knew I would be ostracized even more if I told people the truth."

Are these charges true? Has the church missed an opportunity to minister to its people?

The Ostrich Mentality

Many times the church has hidden its head in the sand and has ignored or denied that Christian young people and adults struggle with sexual activity outside the marriage relationship. Often churches rationalize, "If we don't talk about it, it's not happening." Or they may say, "If we don't talk about it, we won't offend anyone."

However, this mentality only harms the whole church because it communicates that the church is not a place to come for help for crisis pregnancies or abortion counseling. In not talking about issues of sexuality, the church has contributed to the fear many people have of being rejected or ostracized by other Christians.

In not recognizing the need to address these issues, the church has turned away some of the very people who need its help.

Judgment Rather Than Forgiveness

Too often the church has responded to crisis pregnancies or post-abortive women and men with harsh judgment and punitive action rather than helping the people move from guilt to repentance, forgiveness, and restoration. As a result, people in crisis situations are filled with so much guilt and shame that they avoid going to church, or the pregnant woman has an abortion so no one in the church will find out.

In his book *Tired of Trying to Measure Up,* pastoral counselor and author Jeff Van Vonderen writes about the differences between a *healthy* church and a *dysfunctional* church: "In a healthy, functional church system, God is the Source of acceptance, love and value. The pastor, leaders and teachers are there as the helpers and equippers of the other members. Their job, as in a family, is to use their positions of power and authority to equip members for the work of service by serving, building and providing need-meeting experiences, messages and relationships."[1]

In a *dysfunctional* church, "What the people think, how they feel and what they want or need doesn't matter. Their needs go unmet. In these dysfunctional systems the members are there to meet the needs of the leadership. When this happens in the spiritual area, it amounts to spiritual abuse."[2]

Parental Shaming

When parents find out their adolescents are sexually active, they may shame them to the point that communication is destroyed. The adolescents may continue with their sexual activity in secret, losing the support of their parents. These young people often turn to their peers for support, approval, and advice about sexual matters.

If sexual activity results in a crisis pregnancy, some Christian parents push their daughters into having an abortion because they are afraid of what other people in the church will say. The damage to their daughters can be tremendous. One young woman admitted, "I'm very angry at my parents, who call themselves Christians. They made me go through an abortion I didn't want." Christian parents don't realize that forcing their daughter to have an abortion may negatively impact their relationship to her and their relationship to God.

Other Christian parents have taught their children that abortion is wrong, but when their daughter becomes pregnant, they back off and dump the decision in her lap, saying, "It's up to you. We'll support you in whatever decision you make." Perhaps they secretly hope she'll have an abortion so they can all be done with the whole mess. But they don't want the responsibility of telling her to get one. At a time when these young Christian women most need their parents' guidance, they are saddled with the full weight of this life-and-death decision. And when the young women choose to have an abortion, they are left alone to grieve the loss of their child. They are also alone as they carry the shame and guilt of having broken God's commandments.

Christians fear being judged, misunderstood, and shamed. People who are in crisis do not need church members clucking their tongues or pointing fingers of judgment.

BIBLICAL RESPONSES TO SEXUAL SIN

First, the Bible cautions us against judging other people. "Do not judge, or you too will be judged. For in the same way you judge others, you will be judged" (Matt. 7:1–2). When we judge other people, we are usurping God's authority, setting ourselves up to be God.

If anyone had a reason to judge, surely Jesus did when the Pharisees (the judgmental religious leaders) brought to him the woman caught in adultery (John 8:3–11). What was Christ's response? First, he spoke not to the woman but to the Pharisees, who self-righteously brought the woman to him for condemnation. Jesus said, "If any one of you is without sin [no degree of severity mentioned], let him be the first to throw a stone at her" (John 8:7). Christ's comment suggested to the Pharisees that their hidden sins were just as significant as the woman's sin of adultery. Christ's response to the woman was quite gentle. He didn't say to her, "Aha! These men caught you in the act. You know what the Law says about adultery. Confess what you've done, you wicked woman." Instead he said, "Go now and leave your life of sin" (John 8:11).

Another woman, who was notorious for her promiscuous lifestyle received similar caring, nonjudgmental treatment from Jesus. Although Christ knew that the woman at the well had had five husbands and was living with a man she hadn't bothered to marry, the Lord didn't act shocked and he didn't shame or condemn her. Instead, he shifted the emphasis from her sin to the living water—new life he could give. In Christ, she found the true identity and fulfillment she had been searching for through all her unsatisfying sexual relationships.

HINDRANCES TO EFFECTIVE MINISTRY

What has hindered the church from effectively dealing with issues of sexuality, crisis pregnancy, and abortion? What are some blind spots the church needs to examine?

Has the Salt Lost Its Strength?

In the New Testament, Jesus challenges Christians to have a dynamic impact on their culture: "You are the salt of the earth, but if salt has lost its taste—its strength, its quality—how can its saltiness be restored?" (Matt. 5:13–16 AMPLIFIED). This verse calls the church to be a preservative, a force that keeps society from rotting. Have we done that?

Has the church preached and demonstrated sexual values that will keep our world from decaying?

In *Christianity Today,* Charles Colson talks about the "unsalted" nature of today's society: "Vestiges of Christian influence still remain; but those Christian absolutes that have so profoundly shaped Western culture through the centuries are being consciously rejected by the men and women who direct the flow of information and attitudes to popular culture: communicators, educators, writers, and lawyers."[3]

Colson describes the crisis our culture is experiencing: "This . . . is all the more sinister because it is invisible to those who have already become captive to its lie. . . . Freed from the archaic impediments of family, church, and community, these men and women cannot see how their liberty has enslaved them to alienation, betrayal, loneliness, and inhumanity. They have grown so accustomed to the dark, they don't even realize the lights are out."[4]

Jesus instructed Christians to be light to our dark society: "You are the light of the world. A city on a hill cannot be hidden. Neither do people light a lamp and put it under a bowl. Instead they put it on its stand, and it gives light to everyone. . . . Let your light shine before men" (Matt. 5:14–16).

Are We Too Much "of the World"?

Caught up in self-centered pursuits and desires, the church's senses have gradually dulled to the moral decay in our society. Instead of the church influencing our culture as salt and light, many churches have been infiltrated by society's philosophy of self-pleasure and self-fulfillment. James wrote, "Don't you realize that making friends with God's enemies—the evil pleasures of this world—makes you an enemy of God? I say it again, that if your aim is to enjoy the evil pleasure of the unsaved world, you cannot also be a friend of God" (James 4:4 TLB).

The apostle John put it even more strongly. "Do not love the world or anything in the world. If anyone loves the world, the love of the Father is not in him. For everything in the world—the cravings of sinful man, the lust of his eyes and the boasting of what he has and does—comes not from the Father but from the world" (1 John 2:15–16).

To an age in which people are trying to "find themselves," Jesus responds with this counter-cultural command: "Whoever finds his life will lose it, and whoever loses his life for my sake will find it" (Matt. 10:39). To lose your life or to deny yourself is the opposite of today's concept of self-fulfillment, self-actualization, and giving in to sexual desires.

Jesus said, "If anyone would come after me, he must deny himself and take up his cross and follow me. For whoever wants to save his life will lose it, but whoever loses his life for me and for the gospel will save it" (Mark 8:34–35). This is difficult. Many people in the church would rather have freedom to live a lifestyle that pleases their fleshly desires. They adhere to the first part of Galatians 5:13, "You, my brothers, were called to be free" but ignore the last half of the verse, "do not use your freedom to indulge the sinful nature; rather, serve one another in love." The freedom Christ purchased for us through his death on the cross is to be used responsibly with self-control.

Do We Look for Happiness in All the Wrong Places?

Many young people and adults get involved in sexual relationships outside of marriage because they are looking for happiness and fulfillment. Indeed, their desire for pleasure and happiness is so strong, they could be called hedonists.

Hedonism is not all bad, says John Piper, senior pastor

of Bethlehem Baptist Church in Minneapolis. Seeking pleasure is not wrong, as long as we seek our pleasure in God: "You have made known to me the path of life; you will fill me with joy in your presence, with eternal pleasures at your right hand" (Ps. 16:11).

In his book *Desiring God*, Piper defines Christian hedonism as a philosophy of life built on the following five convictions:

1. The longing to be happy is a universal human experience, and it is good, not sinful.
2. We should never try to deny or resist our longing to be happy, as though it were a bad impulse. Instead we should seek to intensify this longing and nourish it with whatever will provide the deepest and most enduring satisfaction.
3. The deepest and most enduring happiness is found only in God.
4. The happiness we find in God reaches its consummation when it is shared with others in the manifold ways of love.
5. To the extent we try to abandon the pursuit of our own pleasure, we fail to honor God and love people. Or, to put it positively: the pursuit of pleasure is a necessary part of all worship and virtue. That is, *The chief end of man is to glorify God BY* [not AND] *enjoying him forever.*[5]

Are We Too Busy to Care?

Another hindrance to the church's effectiveness is busyness. Even Christians who are living morally responsible lives often can get sidetracked by work, continuing education, community and social commitments, and even church-related activities—all of which can hinder our relationship to God, our being salt and light, and our availability to help others in times of need.

When those who are hurting see and experience the love of Christ in the church, we will truly see emotional and spiritual healing. Too often the church is not able to "love the Lord their God with all their heart and their neighbor as themselves" because the church has been caught in the busyness trap. The church has become lukewarm in its love for the Lord and our neighbors.

THE CHURCH AS A HEALTHY, HEALING FORCE

So how can the church respond in a healing way to people in crisis pregnancies and post-abortion experiences? How can the church obey the Bible's commands to love our neighbor and to restore those who have fallen into sin? How can the church be a prophetic voice in our society, addressing issues of sexual immorality and abortion? How can the church equip parents to help their children form sexual values that are in line with biblical directives?

Love God First

We need to realize that before we can reach out to help other people, before we can love our neighbor, we must first love God. In his book, *The Least of These*, Curt Young says, "Throughout the Word of God, we are taught to love God and as a consequence to love our neighbors." He goes on to say, "Our relationship to God is directly indexed by how we treat or regard our neighbor. When we love God, we love our neighbor. When we hate God, we destroy our neighbor. When we're indifferent toward God, we're indifferent toward our neighbor. And who is my neighbor? Anyone within reach of my help."[6]

We will not be able to love our neighbor as God intended unless we spend time with God and become like him. God would rather have us spend time with him than watch us be "busy" for him. Somehow we need to make time in our busy schedules to digest God's Word and let it change us, conform us to the image of Christ.

As individuals and as a church we need to repent of our lukewarm attitudes, our lack of care for others, our hard hearts, and our immorality. In their *Christianity Today* article, "Living in the New Dark Ages," Charles Colson and Ellen Vaughn define this kind of repentance: "Repentance is the process by which we see ourselves, day by day, as we really are: sinful, needy, dependent people. It is the process by which we see God as he is: awesome, majestic, and holy."[7]

Even though the church has lost its first love, it is the only hope in this dark society to bring about true spiritual restoration and healing. Colson and Vaughn see the church as the only instrument that can be used as "outposts of truth, decency, and civilization in the darkening culture around us. For even though the church itself is shot through with an individualism that cripples its witness, even though the church is made up of sinners, it is the one social institution that is still capable of challenging culture by bearing witness to God's transcendent standards of absolute justice and righteousness."[8]

Just as many Old Testament prophets repented on behalf of the children of Israel, we need to repent not only for ourselves but also on behalf of the church and our society. In 2 Chronicles 7:14 God assures us, "If my people, who are called by my name, will humble themselves and pray and seek my face and turn from their wicked ways, then I will hear from heaven and will forgive their sin and will heal their land."

Restore the Fallen

God's Word is clear about the church's responsibility to those who are overcome by sin. In Galatians 6:1–2, Paul says, "If someone is caught in a sin, you who are spiritual should restore him gently. But watch yourself, or you also may be tempted. Carry each other's burdens, and in this way you will fulfill the law of Christ."

How does the church restore the fallen? First, it must be preaching a clear, biblical message. Many people today are hungry to hear godly men and women who have the courage to preach about sin, repentance, and the importance of righteous living. They are hungry to hear preachers who preach about the Lordship of Christ and the sovereignty of God. They are hungry to learn what the Bible says about the struggles they face daily. We need men and women who understand the times and know what to do (1 Chron. 12:32).

Second, the church must be willing to "carry one another's burdens," to come alongside those burdened with sin and its consequences. The church needs to help the burdened find their way back to God and back to wholeness and health, both spiritual and emotional.

Address Issues of Sexuality and Abortion

The church has a unique opportunity—and responsibility—to be a prophetic voice, to speak clearly the Word of God about sexual immorality and abortion. This prophetic voice, first of all, should be heard in the body of Christ itself. The church can't ignore the fact that *Christian* women and men are sexually active and that *Christian* women are becoming pregnant, and having abortions. The church can't ignore its responsibility to do something.

The church's prophetic voice must also be heard in our

society at large, speaking out against media that condone and promote sexual promiscuity, sex education that remains "valueless," and laws that permit abortions. The church can't ignore the fact that our society permits the killing of millions of unborn babies every year.

Curt Young says,

> Armed with the truth of God's Word and the love of Christ, churches are uniquely suited to address the human tragedy of abortion. Without disrupting other vital ministries, churches can effectively deal with the problem of abortion both within their congregations and throughout their communities. People who have suffered abortion can be brought to forgiveness and the knowledge of Christ. Those who face abortion can be taught the better way of choosing life and assisted in doing so. Young adults and others can be directed from the Word of God into an understanding of sexuality and marriage that is both positive and persuasive so they are spared altogether the pain of a crisis pregnancy. Leaders within the community can be taught from Scripture that they are accountable before God to protect the innocent, including the unborn. Finally, they can be encouraged to do so.[9]

Equip Parents

A fourth way the church can influence sexual immorality and abortion is to take seriously its responsibility to equip parents to help their children learn about sexuality. Parents are in a unique position to model healthy sexual relationships. Parents are in an ideal position to promote biblical perspectives about sexuality. The home is the natural place for children to learn about nurturing family relationships, realistic expectations, self-esteem in Christ, and the sanctity of human life.

In *How to Help Your Child Say "No" to Sexual Pressure,* Josh McDowell, a leading Christian spokesperson to young people, talks about the importance of parents teaching their children about sex:

> Proper sex education, or what I prefer to call "life education," is vital and ought to come from parents before it comes from anyone else. Teaching our children about sex is part of our overall responsibility and thrilling privilege as parents to prepare them for life and the proper enjoyment of God's gifts. . . . The first time a parent teaches a child about sex should not be in a formal setting as the child approaches puberty—"the big talk"—but natural opportunities to tell children what they are ready to hear. If you have given your child a good sex education when he or she is growing up, "the big talk" will never be necessary.[10]

Why is it so difficult for parents to talk to their children about sex? McDowell feels that many parents avoid discussing sexual issues because of "discomfort, ignorance, or indifference." The church has a responsibility to teach parents how to communicate with their children about sex. Then when their children face difficult decisions about sexual activity, they will have received the necessary counsel from their parents, supplemented with information from the church. This strong foundation can help kids resist sexual temptation and enable them to come to their parents with such difficult issues as their sexuality, their dating relationships, or struggles with temptation.

One young Christian girl who had an abortion relates her feelings about the closed relationship she had to her parents: "I was so young and so ignorant. Abortion was the 'thing to do' back then, the easy way out, just like having premarital sex was the 'thing to do.' I truly wish I had had a better relationship to my parents or some other loving, caring adult, who would have told me *why* God's plan to wait made so much sense. I hope that I can teach this to other children and young adults, including my own."

The Just-Say-No campaign doesn't go far enough. Without any moral understanding at its foundation, it has little power. The Bible, however, gives us the missing ingredients to make it work. "For the grace of God that brings salvation has appeared to all men. It teaches us to say 'No' to ungodliness and worldly passions, and to live self-controlled, upright and godly lives in this present age" (Titus 2:11–12).

Reach Out to the Hurting and Hopeless

Going back to Jesus' response to the woman at the well, we should also remember that Jesus went out of his way, venturing into hostile territory, to find that woman. When people "drop out" of church, what effort do we make to find out why or bring them back? Most likely, if there's a delicate issue involved, they would be too embarrassed to seek us out and tell us why.

We need to be sensitive and reach out to these young women and men, even if their world seems like hostile territory, to bring healing water to them. Read John 4 again and *feel* Jesus' compassion for the Samaritan woman. Ask him for that kind of compassion in your own life and your own church.

3

Where Have All the Children Gone?

Since the Supreme Court's *Roe* v. *Wade* decision in 1973, over 25 million babies have been aborted in the United States. Obviously this number includes only reported abortions. And the number of abortions has increased every year. In 1985, over 1,588,600 abortions were performed, an increase of 150 percent since 1973. In eight U.S. cities in 1982, more babies were aborted than were born. In 1983, over 12,000 unborn babies twenty-one weeks or older were aborted.[1]

Before abortion became legal nationwide, the national abortion ratio was 180.1 legal abortions per 1000 live births—almost one in five—while the 1987 ratio was 356.1 per 1000 live births—about one in three.[2] And these statistics from the Centers for Disease Control reflect only voluntary reporting by abortion providers who wish to participate in government studies.

Where have all the children gone?

Millions have been aborted.

THE WORTH OF EACH CHILD

Statistics can leave us cold and uninvolved, or they can move us to tears of sadness and anger at this tragic loss of life. What has happened to the values of the American people who approve of this bloodshed? Why do some Christian churches seem to be insensitive to this catastrophe? Perhaps we have forgotten how priceless a child is.

By supporting abortion, the American people, including many Christians, have devalued the worth of each child. They have forgotten that God places great value on each life. He prizes each one of his creations. The message of the creation story is that each of us, including aborted children, was made in the "image of God." And we can agree with the Creator that his work is indeed *good*.

BIBLICAL PERSPECTIVE OF THE UNBORN CHILD

Psalm 139 shows that the developing child is the expression of one of God's greatest creations. As the psalmist says, "You created my inmost being; you knit me together in my mother's womb. I praise you because I am fearfully and wonderfully made; your works are wonderful, I know that full well" (Ps. 139:13–14). The development of this child is called "wonderful" because every baby is a demonstration of God's creative power.

Today debate rages about when life begins, and some people imply that life in the womb has no value before birth. The Word of God clearly shows that even before a woman knows she's pregnant, God knows. He cares for the developing life within the womb.

The psalmist continues, "My frame was not hidden from you when I was made in the secret place. When I was woven together in the depths of the earth, your eyes saw my unformed body. All the days ordained for me were written in your book before one of them came to be" (Ps. 139:15–16). These verses indicate that the child exists when God creates him or her in the womb, not at a later time when the little one has grown to look like a newborn or after the child takes that first breath.

In his booklet *Abortion: A Pastor's Perspective,* John Piper gives his view of Psalm 139 and a similar verse (Job 31:15). Piper states that both Scripture passages

> emphasize *God* as the primary Workman—Nurturer, Fashioner, Knitter, Creator—in this time of gestation. Why is that important? It's important because God is the only One who can create personhood. Mothers and fathers can contribute some impersonal egg and some impersonal sperm, but only God creates independent personhood. So when the Scripture emphasizes that God is the main nurturer and shaper in the womb, it is stressing that what is happening in the womb is the unique work of God, namely, the making of a person. From the Biblical point of view gestation is the unique work of God fashioning personhood.[3]

God deals sovereignly and personally with each unborn life, not only after birth but also before birth.

Scientific Perspective of the Unborn Child

At the instant of conception, a baby's genetic code is present. The basic organs such as kidneys, heart, and brain develop remarkably early. The heart begins beating as early as the eighteenth day. At three weeks, before the woman may even know she is pregnant, her baby possesses the beginnings not only of the heart but also of lungs, eyes, nervous system, spinal cord, and intestines. As early as the sixth week, brain waves are discernible. By forty-five days the baby's skeleton is complete, the unborn can move body and limbs, and tooth buds appear. Before two months in the womb, the baby can grasp an object placed in his or her hand, and the baby's heartbeat can be heard through a stethoscope.[4]

Dr. Paul Rockwell of Troy, New York, witnessed firsthand one of God's smallest creations. Dr. Rockwell describes an eight-week-old fetus, the product of a ruptured tubal pregnancy:

> I was handed what I believed to be the smallest human being ever seen. The embryo sac was intact and transparent. Within the sac was a tiny (one-third inch) human male swimming extremely vigorously in the amniotic fluid, while attached to the wall by the umbilical cord. This tiny human was perfectly developed with long, tapering fingers, feet and toes. It was almost transparent as regards the skin, and the delicate arteries and veins were prominent to the ends of the fingers. The baby was extremely alive.[5]

By two months the tiny person has grown to an inch or more in length. All is now formed, and the changes in the baby's body will be mostly growth in size and refinement of working parts. This tiny one truly looks like a real little person.

But often the little life that has just begun comes to a violent end. In 1986 and 1987, as in previous years, slightly more than half the legal abortions performed were done in the first eight weeks of pregnancy, and nearly 90 percent in the first twelve weeks.[6]

Medical Technology's Perspective of the Unborn Child

Recent advancements in medical technology provide further evidence of the humanity and unique personhood of the unborn child. Thanks to a variety of surgical techniques, instruments, and drug therapy, doctors can treat the unborn child in the womb for a number of health conditions.[7]

Professor Albert W. Liley, developer of the fetal blood-transfusion technique, submitted to the U.S. Senate the following written testimony: "I consider it a bitter irony that just when . . . the fetus arrives on the clinical scene as one who can be cared for medically, there could be such sustained and strenuous effort to make him a social non-entity."[8]

Dr. Bernard Nathanson, who once operated one of the largest abortion clinics in America, makes this observation: "We must courageously face the fact—finally—that human life of a special order is being taken. And since the vast majority of pregnancies are carried successfully to term, abortion must be seen as the interruption of a process that would otherwise have produced a citizen of the world."[9]

While on the one hand medical technology helps us better nurture and treat unborn babies, it has also been responsible for the increase in the number of abortions performed in the past decade. With today's extraordinary diagnostic tools, parents now can know several months into the pregnancy whether or not the baby has any defects or abnormalities. Once they know this information, the parents have to decide if they will bring a deformed child to full term or to abort the child.

Doctors use several techniques to obtain this knowledge. *Ultrasound* photographs bounce high-frequency sound waves off the fetus, reflecting the waves to a recording instrument. These detailed pictures can show abnormalities without exposing the fetus to the danger of X rays. The technique is often used to determine a anencephalic child (one without a brain or having an underdeveloped brain). If parents learn that their baby has no brain, they might be tempted to abort the baby. What sense would there be in having a brainless child who might die shortly after birth?

But some couples, in spite of the anticipated trauma of giving birth to such a child, choose to bring the baby to term. Christian friends of ours, Dan and Denise Campion, found out during the eighth month of Denise's pregnancy that she was carrying a child who had no brain. When they first found out, they wept and grieved and questioned why. But they never considered abortion as an option.

God had prepared Denise months earlier for this tragedy. Early in her pregnancy, during a Bible study, the Lord had impressed on her mind the thought that he knows the number of our days and that he knew the number of days of their baby's life. She knew that God's purpose for their child would be accomplished in the number of days he would give to the child. Some time later, while attending a graveside ceremony, she noticed the headstones of a mother and seven young children. Denise wondered how the woman could have stood the grief of losing seven children. But when she faced the tragic news of her own unborn child, she drew strength from this woman she had never met, feeling that if that woman could make it through the deaths of seven children, she could endure the pain of losing one.

The final month of Denise's pregnancy was traumatic as she and Dan awaited the baby's birth. When Laura was born, they were prepared for her to die right away. But she lived. The doctor told them she might live a few days, so Dan and Denise decided to bring Laura home. To give the baby warmth, they let her sleep between them at night. They spent long hours feeding and taking care of her. People in the church, friends, and family were praying. Laura lived on for weeks.

Dan and Denise kept a bonnet on Laura's head to

prevent people from seeing her deformity. Laura became as precious to them as the other child they had. They loved, nurtured, and prayed for her. One night as Laura slept between them, her breathing became labored. They said, "Laura, go ahead and go if you want to," and she died.

Dan and Denise grieved as if Laura had lived with them for years. They held a funeral for their tiny daughter, and they still keep a picture of Laura on their desks. Throughout this whole ordeal—during the last months of her pregnancy, during the delivery, after they brought Laura home, and during the funeral—God overwhelmed them with his special peace and gave them a calmness they could hardly believe possible.

In cases of severe physical defects such as this, doctors often recommend abortion, but now specialists are experimenting with fetal treatments and surgeries that can help some of these babies.

A second diagnostic procedure is *fetoscopy*. Surgeons insert a needle into the uterus through a thin tube of flexible glass fibers and extract directly from the fetus small samples of skin or blood, which can be examined.

Amniocentesis, another method, gathers information by extracting cells from the amniotic fluid surrounding the fetus. It can determine whether a child has Down's syndrome or any other abnormality: "Chemical analysis of the amniotic cells sometimes reveals fetal defects that will respond to treatment during pregnancy. In the case of abnormalities for which no such prenatal treatment is yet available, early diagnosis and counseling is helpful in preparing the parents for the adjustments they must make in caring for the child after birth. Parents sometimes use the results of this test to determine whether they will keep a fetus if an abnormality exists, or even if the baby is the 'wrong' sex."[10]

While we shudder at the practice of aborting a fetus of "the wrong sex," we can understand the conflict experienced by parents who find that their baby will be born with Down's syndrome or some other disability. How much greater the struggle of a young unwed mother who receives this news.

Heather, a Christian, had already decided to place her baby for adoption, but when she discovered that the baby had Down's syndrome, she struggled with her decision. When the infant was born, doctors told her the baby also had several other severe physical problems that would require surgery. Fearing that no one would want to adopt her baby boy, Heather felt responsible to take the baby home and care for him herself.

But soon a young Christian couple expressed interest in the baby. They had always wanted a Down's syndrome child because there had been one in the family, and they had a special love for such children. They knew the risks; they knew the baby might not live. When the baby was three months old, he had extensive surgery. Not only did the baby survive the surgery, but he also developed more than anyone thought he could, becoming a cheerful, healthy child.

Heather had peace to place her baby with this couple for adoption. Someone wanted her child. God had miraculously provided the right parents, and now the little boy is doing well—loved by his new parents and accepted by the church family. This child, who by the world's standards would have been aborted, has been a special gift of life.

If your doctor were to advise you to have an abortion on medical grounds, what would you do? In their book *Baby Mayfield,* Larry and Diane Mayfield describe the dilemma they faced when Diane began experiencing excruciating back pain from a large piece of disc that had broken off and had become imbedded in a nerve. She endured numerous X rays, tests, surgery, and strong narcotic pain killers before she realized that she had been pregnant throughout all of the treatment.

Her Christian, pro-life doctor advised Diane to abort. "Few doctors are as opposed to abortion as I am, morally and religiously," he told her. "I'm speaking to you medically, practically. . . . Your baby was four to six inches away from that X-ray machine at a very critical stage in his development. His brain stem and nervous system were being developed. The odds are that we have caused severe damage."[11]

Because of their Christian convictions, the Mayfields refused abortion, but their decision wasn't easy. They couldn't help but wonder what would happen if they gave birth to a deformed child and Diane, whose back was in no shape to support childbirth, was further injured. Larry was already playing the role of Mr. Mom since Diane had been incapacitated. Was it fair to ask him to take care of two invalids for the rest of his life?

After much struggle with the reality that their child could be born handicapped, they trusted God to give them the strength, grace, and compassion they would need. In faith they took Psalm 139 as their text and "claimed the truth that the body that was being formed within Diane was fearfully and wonderfully made, that it was being knit together in secret in her innermost parts. They made it a point to pray for that unborn child every day during her pregnancy, specifically asking God to do His perfect will in creating every minute detail. From fingernails and tiny toes to kidneys, liver, limbs, and hair, they prayed and prayed as the days rolled by."[12]

And after a very difficult delivery, they found their son completely whole, totally healthy.

FACING REALITY

The statistics and thoughts in this chapter about the specialness of each of God's creations are not meant to add more guilt to the women and men who have had abortion experience. But an essential part of the healing process is to understand the sanctity of each human life, especially the life of the child who has been aborted.

People who work with women and men struggling with a crisis pregnancy or a past abortion need to be able to share this information with those they are counseling.

4

Why Do Women Have Abortions?

In 1990, the Conquerors ministry conducted a survey, a personal inventory, of women who had had abortions. Their responses to the many questions have helped us understand the issues they have faced before, during, and after their abortion experience. One of the things they have helped us understand is why they had their abortions. Many of them had several reasons, but their responses fall into these seven categories:

1. Pressure from parents, husband, boyfriend, or pro-choice counselor
2. Fear of having other people find out about the pregnancy and of bringing shame on family and self
3. Bad timing: too young, in school, financially unable
4. Stressful circumstances: abusive home situation, poor environment
5. Possible deformity
6. Selfishness: interferes with lifestyle, not the right sex
7. Support for the abortion position

WOMEN FEEL PRESSURED INTO ABORTIONS

Many women are personally opposed to abortion, but when they face a crisis pregnancy, they are pressured by other people to get an abortion.

Pressure from Parents

Many times a young, unmarried woman's parents pressure her to abort the baby. Some parents exert pressure for selfish reasons; they worry about what other people will think. They fear their reputation will be ruined. Other parents have a genuine concern for their daughter and feel abortion is the best solution for her.

Regardless of the parents' reasons, placing pressure on their pregnant daughter does not help her crisis. It may make them feel better, but their daughter still may feel that an abortion is very wrong.

Most women who are pushed into an abortion by their parents hold anger and resentment toward them for years. The following excerpts from the Conquerors personal inventory surveys show the feelings of some of the women who were pressured and even forced to have an abortion:

- "I was a minor, and my parents made the decision. Their reasons were: I was too young to have a child. 'It' would interfere with my finishing high school and college. 'It' would ruin my life. 'It' would ruin our family's reputation. 'It' would ruin 'its' father's life and education. We couldn't support 'it,' and our parents wouldn't help. I fought as best I could, but I felt overwhelmed and powerless. I hoped that my instincts of how horrendous the experience was would turn out to be wrong. For twelve years I tried to convince myself they were right, but I failed."

Pressure from Husband or Boyfriend

One of most powerful forms of pressure is from the husband who has promised to love and cherish his wife and protect his family. A wife often feels a duty to her husband— to listen to him, to trust his judgment in difficult matters, and to protect his children. When a husband puts pressure on his wife to abort their child, the relationship suffers, communication is broken down, love and trust is destroyed, and other children in the family suffer.

Women who are very dependent on their boyfriends or husbands for love, approval, and self-esteem often feel strongly committed to their wishes in a crisis pregnancy. Many times these women are fearful that their husbands or boyfriends will leave if they don't submit to their wishes. The following stories describe the pain and anguish women feel when their husband or boyfriend is pressuring her to have an abortion:

- "The doctor met with my husband and me and showed us some pictures of fetal development. He said we had to hurry and decide because I would have to have the abortion within a certain time limit. The doctor asked if we wanted to go ahead with the abortion. My husband said yes, and my yes followed although everything in my heart and mind screamed no. Within a couple of days arrangements were made. My husband dropped me off at the hospital. The whole abortion experience was awful emotionally. After the abortion was started, I wanted it stopped, but I couldn't communicate that to the medical people. I knew already it was too late. It was very traumatic to have the doctor search through a pan for my child's body parts, to make sure he had gotten everything. From that point on, I felt emotionally dead. Our marriage suffered because of the strain of the abortion. I no longer trusted my husband, and I no longer felt close to him. This made me very sad because I was so much in love with him before the abortion. I felt betrayed because I thought he loved me. I felt so bad that I had allowed my child to be killed. I was upset that I wasn't a stronger person. Emotionally, I withdrew from my husband and also from my daughter to some extent."

Pressure from Pro-choice Counselors

● "When I became pregnant, I felt hopeless. I wanted to keep the baby, date my boyfriend, and eventually marry him. The counselor I talked to was very pro-abortion. She did not explain to me all of the options. Therefore, I didn't have accurate information with which to make a decision. I wish I had received more information about adoption, for instance. I wish someone had just pushed that information on me. I wanted someone to say, 'No, you shouldn't do this. God would not approve.'"

FEAR

Other women said they had abortions because they were afraid to let other people know that they had become pregnant. They were afraid of judgment and rejection by their parents or the church. They also were afraid that their pregnancy would bring shame to themselves and their family.

Fear of Having Other People Know About the Pregnancy

Many times women have abortions because they are afraid their parents or other people will find out they were pregnant. These women do not want their families and friends to have negative thoughts about them. They are afraid that their parents would judge them or ostracize them.

- "The main reason I had an abortion was because I didn't want my mother to find out that I had been sexually active. I wanted my mother to think I was a 'good girl.' The shame I feel is that my mother doesn't know about my abortion. I don't think I could ever tell her."

Fear of Bringing Shame on Self, Family, and Church

Christian women have an even deeper struggle when they become pregnant out of wedlock. Not only are they fearful of displeasing parents and ruining their reputation, but they are also fearful of bringing shame on the name of Christ and the life they are trying to live among other Christians. The church has difficulty talking about sex, pregnancy, and abortion. Imagine the shame a woman has when she has to admit to all three. Many times these women suffer alone as they try to hide their shame from the church, their Christian parents, their Christian friends, and ultimately, from God.

- "I was scared when I found out I was pregnant. I was very involved in my church and felt I couldn't possibly admit I had been sexually active—and even worse, that I was pregnant. I didn't think anyone would understand. I didn't want to disappoint my parents, either. I had failed to be the perfect daughter, Christian, friend, and church leader everyone thought I was. I panicked. I thought I could 'get rid' of the problem and deny it ever happened. My boyfriend was equally scared and was concerned about his image, so he encouraged me to have the abortion.

- "I was single and frightened to death. My father was a pastor, and I felt that he wouldn't be able to handle the fact that I was pregnant. I felt that I was bringing shame on the family, especially to my father. Ironically, the fact that I had an abortion would be more upsetting to him than my being pregnant. Unfortunately, I never thought of that at the time."

BAD TIMING

Other women said they had abortions because they felt their pregnancy came at the wrong time. They were in high school and felt they were too young to be a parent. They felt a baby would interfere with their schooling. Or they may have felt they were financially unable to care for a baby. In desperation, they saw abortion as the solution.

- "I chose to have an abortion because I was young and in college. The pregnancy came at an inconvenient time. No one offered me an alternative. I thought about adoption, but I felt it would be difficult to give my baby away. At the time of the abortion, I thought of my baby as a bunch of cells. I convinced myself of that. I wanted to get rid of my problem as soon as I could, no matter what I would have to live with for the rest of my life. Sometimes I wish someone in the abortion clinic just would have told me that social services in our city could have helped me through my pregnancy.

LIVING IN STRESSFUL CIRCUMSTANCES

For women living under extremely stressful circumstances—abusive home situation, incest, divorce, single parenting—abortion can seem to be an easy solution to a problem. A crisis pregnancy at this time is overwhelming. Women are unable to make wise decisions for their babies and themselves. This was the plight of the woman in the following story:

- "At the time of the abortion I was a divorced, single parent of one. My partner of seven months was in treatment for alcoholism. I *had* been using birth control. The conception was a horrible mistake. I wasn't sure if our relationship was permanent, and I could not afford another child on my own. The father could not make a commitment because of his own personal problems. I was experiencing a lot of morning sickness and cramping. As the holidays approached, the anxiety was more than I could bear. Although my partner initially said he didn't want me to abort, he was very relieved when I announced that I had decided to."

POSSIBLE DEFORMITY

Other women indicated they had abortions because they were told their baby would be born with a deformity. Many doctors encourage women to abort so they won't have to care for a deformed child for the rest of their lives.

- "The medication I had been taking to treat my allergies had been known to cause birth defects. When I had an ultrasound at nine weeks and found that the baby had birth defects in the spine and heart, I elected to have an abortion."

Counselor Madeline Pecora Nugent, author of *Having Your Baby When Others Say No,* in a paper called "Letter on

Abortion of Handicapped Babies," says that parents who are faced with the option of aborting a baby with handicaps or special needs should keep the following points in mind:

1. Afraid of malpractice suits, doctors sometimes recommend abortions if the baby *might* be deformed or handicapped.
2. Society pressures fearful parents to abort a handicapped child, making them feel that caring for the child would require heroic efforts, and they may not be equal to the task.
3. Rather than encouraging parents to care for a handicapped child, professionals sometimes reinforce the parents' fear that they would not be able to handle the emotional strain.
4. In our cost-conscious and productivity-conscious society, friends may argue that a special-needs child will be more of a financial burden than a "normal" child.[1]

SELFISHNESS

Several women indicated they had had abortions for purely selfish reasons.

- "The reason for my abortion was pure selfishness. At the time, I considered myself a 'liberated' woman, independent. I had control over my own life. I was not accountable to anyone."

- "After having given birth to three girls, we discovered our fourth child was also female. My husband was crushed and angry. He really wanted a son. We decided to abort the female and try again for a male."

SUPPORT FOR THE ABORTION POSITION

Some women indicated that they had an abortion because they believed it was the right thing to do. They fully supported the abortion position.

Some women make an intellectual decision that if they do get pregnant, abortion is the answer for them. After listening to pro-choice teaching they have received in schools and from their peers, abortion seems the best solution. Even though the decision to face an abortion may be difficult, they set their mind on it and appear not to struggle with the emotional pain that other women have experienced following their abortion.

- "I'm not a typical post-abortion case because I knew that having an abortion was the right thing to do. I never felt guilt or remorse. When I found out I was pregnant, I worried only about where to go. The clinic took care of everything. I remember mostly a sense of relief, and I hoped I had learned my lesson. A girlfriend went with me to give me emotional support. I'm a very independent person who is not overly emotional. I need to be in total control of my life, and I'm willing to do what's necessary to not let fate determine my future. I realize that not many women feel as I do, but I have never been sorry."

PEOPLE WANT "UNWANTED" CHILDREN

Many of the reasons women have abortions is that for a variety of reasons, they didn't want their unborn babies. In the fifteen years I have worked in social services, I have worked both with women and men who have agonized over unwanted pregnancies as well as with couples who have agonized because they want children so much, but they are unable to conceive.

When women face crisis pregnancies, they need to ask themselves, Is my baby unwanted just because I don't want it? Is there someone out there who does want my baby?

New Life Family Services has a three-year waiting list of adoptive couples who want a baby. The only reason the waiting list is not longer at our agency and the other placement agencies in Minneapolis (which have seven-year waiting lists) is that we have had to quit taking so many applications. There simply are not enough babies for those who are waiting.

In their book, *Baby Mayfield*, Larry and Diane Mayfield, with writer Jerry B. Jenkins, tell of the Mayfields' struggle with infertility and subsequent adoption of their first child, Tracie, in 1970. "Ahead of the abortion epidemic by three years, they had little trouble effecting a private adoption, which was hardly the case three and a half years later when they hoped to adopt again."

Diane remembers being "all but laughed from the room" when they talked to the adoption agency the second time. Larry says, "We were virtually told, 'Forget it.' We were made to feel stupid and naïve for even thinking we could adopt another baby. We left with our heads spinning, thrilled that we had gotten Tracie when we did."[2]

In view of the long waiting lists at adoption agencies, is it too farfetched to assume that for the 1.5 million children that are aborted each year, there are at least 1.5 million couples yearning to adopt these children?

PART II

The Effects of Abortion

5

Who Has Been Affected by Abortions?

Abortions affect women and men of all ages, races, educational backgrounds, and religions. While society readily acknowledges that the unborn child and its mother are affected by abortion, it is less aware of the other people affected by abortion: fathers, parents, children, grandparents, siblings, and friends. And we don't want to ignore the effect of abortion on the abortion professionals. Part II will explore the various physical, emotional, and spiritual effects that abortion has on these women and men.

This chapter will look closely at the people themselves, the women and men who are affected by abortion. The first section will examine what statistics tell us about the women who have abortions. The data given in the first part of this chapter were gathered from four sources: the Conquerors study, national statistics, the Women Exploited by Abortion (WEBA) study, and a study done by Anne Speckhard.

THE SOURCES

The Conquerors study data was gathered in 1990 from a five-page personal inventory completed by sixty-eight women

67

who have had abortions. The women had various types of abortions, at various places, and at various gestation times during the pregnancy. Half of the survey participants responded to an ad in ten Minnesota newspapers asking for women who had had abortions to be part of a research project. The other participants were either women who had contacted New Life Family Services to find out more about the Conquerors post-abortion groups or women who already had been in the Conquerors program. The personal inventory asked questions about demographic data as well as emotional, spiritual, and physical symptoms of abortion. This chapter will address the demographic data, while the next three chapters will discuss their comments about the physical, emotional, and spiritual dynamics of their abortion experience. Many of the women not only replied to the inventory questions but also wrote lengthy explanations of their abortion experience.

The national statistics are based on the government's studies through the center for chronic Disease Prevention and Health Promotion.[1] The data is from 1987; this is the most recent study available.

The WEBA study was done in 1986 by researcher David C. Reardon in cooperation with the national organization, Women Exploited by Abortion (WEBA). Reardon studied a group of 252 women and discussed his findings in his book *Aborted Women Silent No More*.[2]

The Speckhard study was conducted in 1984 by Anne Speckhard, who has a Ph.D. in psychology. Speckhard's study included thirty women who were identified as having a chronic and long-term stress reaction to their abortion experiences. Dr. Speckhard reported her findings in her book *The Psycho-Social Stress Following Abortion.*[3]

DEMOGRAPHIC DATA OF WOMEN WHO HAD ABORTIONS

The following charts, statistics, and interpretations will help us understand more about women who have had abortions. In several cases the comparisons will not include identical categories (for instance, the Conquerors study divided the "unmarried" women category into two parts— "unmarried, single" and "unmarried, divorced"—while the national statistics used only an "unmarried" category), but the comparisons are nonetheless helpful.

MARITAL STATUS

Conquerors study		National statistics		WEBA study[4]	
Married	9%	Married	27%	Married	18%
Unmarried, Single	82%	Unmarried	73%	Unmarried, Single	67%
Unmarried, Separated/				Unmarried, Engaged	6%
Divorced	9%			Unmarried, Separated/	
				Divorced	6%

All of the studies reflected similar percentages of women who were single when they aborted, but the WEBA study and the national study showed more married women who had aborted. Most studies agree that single women have abortions because of their fear of single parenting.

There are similarities between the studies of the twenty-year-old to twenty-nine-year-old women who have had abortions, but the Conquerors, WEBA, and Speckhard studies show a greater percentage of teenage women who have had abortions. The Conquerors study revealed that 11 percent of the women had their first abortions between the ages of fourteen and sixteen.

AGE AT TIME OF FIRST ABORTION

Conquerors study		National statistics		WEBA study		Speckhard study	
Ages 14–19	39%	Ages 17–19	30%	Ages 15–19	42%	Ages 14–18	31%
20–28	52%	20–29	55%	20–29	50%	19–21	23%
31–36	9%	30 & over	16%	30 & over	8%	22–30	39%
						31–36	8%

We may speculate about the reasons why the teenagers in the three studies had more abortions than the national average. Some of the women who had abortions as teenagers may be experiencing more emotional stress from their abortion, thus coming to Speckhard, Conquerors, or WEBA for help. The teenagers, perhaps more vulnerable because of their age, may have been pressured by parents or boyfriends to have an abortion.

WEEKS OF GESTATION FOR FIRST ABORTION

Conquerors study		National statistics		Speckhard study	
8 wks. and under	43%	8 wks. and under	50.4%	11 wks. or less	50%
9–10 wks.	25%	9–10 wks.	26.0%	12–23 wks.	46%
11–15 wks.	23%	11–15 wks.	18.6%	24 wks. and over	4%
16–25 wks.	9%	16 wks. and over	5.0%		

The Speckhard study and national statistics showed more abortions performed at an earlier gestation date than the Conquerors study.

The Conquerors study asked women to classify themselves in terms of religion or denominational affiliation. Only 94.1 percent of the women filled out this part of the inventory, but these are their responses:

CONQUERORS STUDY OF RELIGIOUS AFFILIATION

Agnostic/no faith	3.1%
Catholic	11%
Evangelical*	35.6%
Baptist	4.7%
Pentecostal	4.7%
Evangelical Free	3.1%
Assemblies of God	3.1%
Nondenominational	7.8%
Covenant	1.6%
Full Gospel	1.6%
Nonspecific	9.0%
Lutheran	25%
Episcopal	1.6%
Methodist	1.6%
Christian	
(denomination not noted)	14%

The Conquerors study evaluated the spiritual symptoms of the women, and women who had religious faith wanted to be a part of the study.

TYPE OF ABORTION**

Conquerors study		National statistics (1987)		Speckhard study	
Vacuum aspiration	72%	Vacuum aspiration	93.3%	Vacuum aspiration	65%
Saline injection	6%	Saline injection	1.3%	Saline injection	12%
D&C or D&E†	11%	D&C or D&E	3.7%	D&C or D&E	23%
Unknown	11%				

*Note the large number of evangelical women who have had an abortion. Others listed under mainline denominations or "Christian" may also consider themselves evangelicals, making this statistic difficult to evaluate.

**For a thorough explanation of what is involved in each of these procedures, see chapter 7.

†/D&C is dilatation & curettage; D&E is dilatation & evacuation.

Quite a disparity exists between the abortion procedures cited in the national study and the Conquerors and Speckhard studies. Compared to the Speckhard and Conquerors studies, the national statistics show a 20 percent to almost 30 percent increase in the use of the vacuum aspiration method and a corresponding decrease in the D&C, D&E, and saline procedures.

Part of the cause for this disparity is that the Conquerors study was based on women who had abortions an average of ten to fifteen years ago. At that time doctors used more diverse methods. Perhaps a more accurate comparison could be made between the Conquerors abortion-procedure statistics and the 1972 national study statistics.

TYPE OF ABORTION

Conquerors study		National statistics (1972)	
Vacuum aspiration	72%	Vacuum aspiration	65.2%
Saline injection	6%	Saline injection	10.4%
D&C or D&E	11%	D&C or D&E	23.4%
		Hysterotomy/	
Unknown	11%	hysterectomy	0.6%
		Other	0.5%

Note the much higher incidence of saline injection abortions in the 1972 national statistics. The 1987 statistics reflect the convenience of the vacuum method and the negative results of the saline abortion procedure, which many times produces a live, salt-burned baby. Delivering such babies can cause trauma for the aborting women, nurses, and doctors. The D&C and D&E procedures are also used less often now because the abortionist has to scrape the wall of the uterus and cut the baby's body into pieces. This, too, can cause the doctor trauma.

REPEAT ABORTIONS

Conquerors study		National statistics	
1 previous abortion	10%	1 previous abortion	70%
3 or more previous abortions	1.3%	2 previous abortions	16%
		3 or more previous abortions	14%

Speckhard study		WEBA study	
1 previous abortion	78%	more than 1 previous abortion	24%
2 previous abortions	13%		
3 or more previous abortions	8%		

According to the national statistics, about 33 percent of all abortions are performed on women who have had previous abortions. The relatively low repeat-abortion rate indicated by the Conquerors study reflects the fact that many women had their abortions five to fifteen years ago (over 50 percent of the women in the Conquerors study had their abortions ten years ago). The Conquerors study lower repeat-abortion rate may also reflect the fact that many of the women had religious values and either renewed their relationship to Christ or became Christians since their abortion experience. Many of them are deeply opposed to having an abortion now.

One woman who attended the Conquerors group had had four abortions. She now deeply regrets her decisions. Before coming to Conquerors, she tried to numb her abortion pain by drinking and using drugs heavily. She also became anorexic and tried to commit suicide four times. The reality of taking the life of her four children dawned on her when she was in church, attending a funeral of a child who had died:

> Sitting in that church, surrounded by people weeping for the pain of the young parents there, Elisa wept. She wept for them, but she also wept for herself and her children. "It was so real to me for the first time. I

pictured four children sitting in the Lord's lap. One little girl looked just like me. And she said, 'Jesus, why is Mommy crying?'" Two weeks later while she was standing by her kitchen sink, the horror of what she had done overwhelmed her. "I said, 'God, do you *realize* what I really did? Do you know what I did, God?' . . . Now when I look back, there is a real sadness," says Elisa. "I regret that I never held my children in my arms. I'll hold them in Heaven," she adds, smiling slightly.[5]

WHO ELSE IS AFFECTED BY ABORTION?

Abortion affects not only the mothers of aborted babies but also the fathers, surviving siblings, grandparents, and abortion providers. Each of these people suffers his or her own negative psychological and spiritual consequences.

Men and Abortion

The impact of abortion on men has been greatly neglected by the helping community. Men have played three roles in the abortion experience: some men have pressured their sexual partner to seek an abortion; other men have fought against the abortion; and still other men have refused to be part of the decision, saying to their sexual partners, "Do what you want." (Chapter 10 will share the stories of men in each of these situations.)

Regardless of what their role was in the abortion, most men will be affected in some way. As with women, some men are affected immediately, and others don't realize the impact for a number of years.

Stanhope reports that Arthur B. Shostak, a basically pro-choice sociologist at Drexel University, interviewed a thousand men on university campuses and at abortion-clinic waiting rooms, and Shostak discovered that many men struggle greatly with their abortion experience. "Eighty-one percent of the men surveyed said they have thought about their unborn children and that, generally, they felt isolated (at the abortion clinic), angry with themselves (for letting it happen) and, by and large, concerned for the physical and emotional well-being of their partners."[6]

Stanhope paraphrases Dr. Vincent Rue, executive director of the Sir Thomas More Clinic (Downey, California), saying that "Men . . . will often experience persistent day and night dreams about the child; considerable guilt, remorse and sadness; the end of the relationship with his partner; and potential aggression via self-abuse."[7]

At a time when men have been more involved in the parenting of their children, they ironically have less to say about whether their unborn child will be aborted. With women fighting for their "rights" over their own bodies, they often don't even discuss an unwanted pregnancy with their husbands or boyfriends. When a father is not consulted and the abortion is performed, many times he feels anger, betrayal, powerlessness, and a loss of trust. Ultimately, when his trust relationship with the mother has been damaged, the relationship usually is destroyed.

Siblings and Abortion

Young children are often aware that their mother is pregnant or that she has had an abortion, even when they are not told about it. Many times children overhear their parents talking about having an abortion or about an aborted child. Some parents believe their children are too young to understand. Others think that if the children know about an abortion, they will forget about it. But children don't forget.

Children may react a number of ways when they find

out their mother has aborted a brother or sister. They may feel despair, confusion, and especially fear: fear of their mother, fear that the parents may get rid of them next, fear of the world in general, fear that they may be responsible in some way for the abortion of their sibling.

Andrea, who is thirteen, was so affected by the news of her mother's abortion experience seven years before Andrea was born that she wrote a paper for school about it. She titled the paper, "One in Heaven."

> I found out about the abortion two years ago. My parents sat my brother and me down and talked to us about it. When I first heard about it, I cried. I was sad and angry. I wasn't angry at any person. I just couldn't understand why this had to happen to *my* family. Our family was supposed to be so perfect. This couldn't be happening to me. I thought that things like that only happened to other families. I guess I was wrong.

> I love that older sister or brother whom I never will see on earth. I wish I could tell her how I feel and tell her about our family.

> Through this experience I learned more about abortion, and I am even more against it. I don't believe people when they tell me that there is no victim in abortion. One abortion can affect the lives of the family *and* friends of the one who had the abortion.

> I'm not mad at my mom and dad. I love my parents, and I know that they wouldn't hurt me for the world. I'm not glad that my mom had an abortion, but I am glad that she can help others now who have had abortions.

> I felt sad for a long time, and I still do, but God has done a lot through this experience. Letting him have control hasn't been easy. It has been scary. I don't want

to have to deal with the pain, but I know God can't work through me unless he has control of all my life. If anyone wonders how many people are in my family, I have a mom, a dad, and older brother, and "one in heaven."

Andrea's mother told her children about the the abortion because the Lord had given her a public ministry, helping other women through their post-abortion trauma. Each woman and man will handle this decision differently. If parents feel their children are mature enough to handle the news or if parents plan to speak publicly about their abortion experience, then they should plan to tell their children.

Dr. Phillip Ney, a psychiatrist and professor at the University of Otago in New Zealand, published a report showing the direct relationship between the rise in the number of abortions and an increased incidence of child abuse. Ney states that "the violent act of abortion, compounded by the mother's guilt and unresolved grief following an abortion, lessens her instinctual restraint against harming her other children, thus leading to more child abuse. Ney also states that the surviving children in the family often feel a mixture of guilt and anger known as the 'survivor syndrome,' because they feel guilty that they survived while the other child did not."[8]

Grandparents and Abortion

New Life Family Services has had many calls from people asking if the counselors would speak with their pregnant daughter who is set on having an abortion. The unborn baby's grandparents feel helpless as their daughter chooses to abort their unborn grandchild. They struggle with anger and bitterness toward their daughter. Their relationship becomes strained and may never be the same unless they can learn to forgive her and grieve the loss of their grandchild.

After receiving such a call from a distraught mother, I met with the parents and their fifteen-year-old daughter. Together we looked at the alternatives for the daughter and unborn baby. After the meeting, I didn't hear from the family for a week, so I called them to see what the daughter had decided. When the mother answered the phone, I could tell she was depressed. She told me that her daughter had talked her into taking her to have an abortion the day before. The mother was emotionally and physically sick over the loss of her unborn grandchild. I tried to comfort her, but she was despairing. As I hung up, my heart grieved with her over the loss of her grandchild.

One grandmother tells how her grief and loss affected her:

A Grandmother's Story

"Comfort is not available for those who mourn a loved one lost in secret—a loved one so small it had not ever been seen. Yet it is a loss we will never be able to forget—a child who might have wondered at the splendor and lights of Christmas, who might have lain in our arms lulled to sleep by 'Silent Night,' who would have toddled to us, thrilled with new possessions, shiny toys, and soft cuddly things to love. . . . Even if the world does not know we are grandmothers, we still can love the little ones who were, but are not visible to us. And if we can reach their mothers—our daughters—whose lives are injured even more deeply than our own, we can take them in our arms. We can tell them that we understand and love them still, bearing all our own guilt for failing to meet the needs that drove them to the decision that stole their children and injured them. But most of all, we can love our daughters and use our pain to ease their guilt and sadness and to prevent this tragedy from ever happening again to anyone."[9]

Abortion Providers

In a *Los Angeles Daily Journal* article entitled, "Fewer Doctors Performing Abortions," Gina Kolata discusses how abortion affects health professionals:

> Many obstetricians and gynecologists acknowledge that they feel great conflict about abortion.
>
> A doctor who is an administrator at the National Institutes of Health . . . said she used to carry them out because she felt strongly that abortions should be available.
>
> But, she said, she had to prepare herself emotionally each time, and she often had a sleepless night before a scheduled abortion.
>
> "It's a very tough thing for a gynecologist to do," she said. The emotions it arouses are so strong . . . that doctors "don't talk to each other about it."
>
> The doctor said she was performing an abortion on a 30-year-old doctor after she herself had just had a miscarriage.
>
> She had been trying for seven years to become pregnant. After the abortion, she said, "I just collapsed on the floor," overcome by her emotions.[10]

Abortion procedures also take a toll on nurses. As president of the National Association of Pro-Life Nurses, registered nurse Marilyn Derby has talked with many nurses who have worked with abortions. She found a "tremendous strain between the training a nurse receives as a preserver of life and the dehumanizing work she performs assisting an abortionist. . . . Compared to a nurse's role when there is a 'spontaneous abortion' or miscarriage, where she consoles the woman (mother) of the loss of a 'wanted child,' here she is forced to 'stuff' her natural response of sympathy and grief to a response of relief for the mother (woman) for becoming 'unpregnant.'"[11]

Many nurses experience trauma in having to reassemble all the dismembered body parts of the fetus after a dilatation and evacuation abortion (see chapter 6 for explanations of the various methods used in abortions) to ensure that "they got it all" and to prevent further complications. In saline abortions "the abortionist leaves the aftermath to the nurse, who frequently delivers a dead or dying 'fetus.' She has to minister to a hysterical mother and dispose of a body similar in size and development to 'preemies' who [would be] rushed to a neo-natal intensive care unit. Only this baby is taken away in a bedpan and set aside to die."[12]

Although many nurses even quit their profession, they carry the emotional scars with them. "Symptoms include 'flashbacks,' nightmares, depression, sleep disorders, suicide, drug and/or alcohol abuse, and other self-destructive behavior."[13]

Abortion has many victims—not only the women and babies but the husbands, boyfriends, grandparents, and siblings. Even the nurses and doctors who do the abortions unwittingly become victims. The following chapters will examine more closely the physical, psychological, and spiritual consequences of abortion.

6

Physical Effects of Abortion
RUTH A. BOLTON, M.D.

What is involved in an abortion, and what are the physical complications of abortion? To answer these questions, I've asked Dr. Ruth Bolton to review the physiological effects of abortion. Dr. Bolton's experiences as unit director of the North Memorial Family Practice Residency and as an assistant professor at the University of Minnesota, Department of Family Practice and Community Health uniquely qualify her to write this chapter.

The 1973 *Roe* v. *Wade* decision to legalize abortion rested partially on the statistics of deaths due to illegal abortions compared to mortality rates from childbirth. Today, however, a great deal of evidence refutes the data used in this court decision.

A WORD ABOUT THE DATA

Dr. Bernard Nathanson, in his bestseller *Aborting America,* admits that the reported five to ten thousand women per year dying from back-alley abortions before 1973 is "totally

81

false."[1] Dr. Nathanson was at one time head of the world's largest abortion clinic. In his book he explained that he and others circulated these false figures in 1972 in order to bring about legal abortion. In 1972 (the year before abortion on demand was legalized), only thirty-nine abortion-related deaths nationwide were officially reported. Admittedly, if back-alley abortions are not reported, deaths connected with them certainly would not be. However, there is no substantiation whatsoever for the reports of five to ten thousand deaths per year.

Abortion is the most commonly performed outpatient procedure in the United States. More than 1.6 million abortions are performed each year, yet actual statistics regarding complications with these abortions are rarely publicized.[2] In January 1989, former U.S. Surgeon General C. Everett Koop cited two specific reasons for the inability to obtain accurate abortion-complication data:

1. Up to one-half of all abortions are done in freestanding clinics where records are not kept.
2. Fifty percent of women who have had an abortion deny having one when questioned.[3]

Therefore, any data on abortion complications are skewed, and accurate reporting becomes an impossibility. Abortion clinics may do little follow-up with the patients after the actual procedure. Office physicians and emergency-room personnel are often unaware of a recent abortion experience when a woman comes to them for treatment. And even if the patient tells the physician about the abortion, her complications are usually not reported to the abortion clinic. Understandably, the more trouble a patient has after an abortion, the less likely she is to return to that clinic for follow-up care.

Beyond that, it is clear that comparing abortion-related

mortality to childbirth-related deaths is statistically impossible. Maternal abortion-related deaths are measured in relation to 100,000 abortions performed. Maternal mortality is the number of deaths per 100,000 *live births*.[4] The numerator in the latter equation includes *all* maternal deaths, including abortions, stillbirths, miscarriages, and ectopic (tubal) pregnancies. The 100,000 denominator of live births excludes those pregnancies that do not result in a live birth, therefore artificially inflating the number of maternal deaths.

Also, it is statistically inappropriate to compare two sets of data (maternal vs. abortion) if one set (abortion) is included in the other. Deaths from long-term abortion complications are not recorded under abortion mortality but under other categories including childbirth. Any complications from second- and third-trimester abortions resulting in live births are reported as complications of childbirth and not from abortions.

Because of these errors in statistical reporting and because no accurate means to collect abortion data has been found, we should carefully scrutinize any report of abortion statistics. In an attempt to eliminate any bias on either side of the debate, this overview attempts to report only strict medical data about the known medical aspects of abortion.

PHYSIOLOGICAL ASPECTS OF ABORTION

Medically, *abortion* is defined as "spontaneous or intentional interruption of a pregnancy." That definition is fairly clear.

What is not clear, however, is defining when life of the unborn actually begins. Legal precedents have helped make the definition more clear. In a case involving frozen embryos, Tennessee Circuit Court Judge W. Dale Young declared that "human life begins at the moment of conception [union of the sperm and egg]."[5] Biblical descriptions of life certainly support this judge's decision. The Bible definitely speaks of *life* in the womb. In Psalm 51:5 David admitted that he was sinful from the time of his conception.

Medically, *gestation* is defined as "the number of weeks from the first day of the last menstrual period" and not from conception; the last menstrual period is measurable, whereas the moment of conception is more difficult to pinpoint. A full-term (forty-week) pregnancy is divided into three trimesters. Statistics show that 89 percent of all abortions are done in the first twelve weeks of pregnancy (first trimester).[6] A baby is viable, capable of living outside the uterus, at the beginning of the third trimester. Many babies have lived when they were born toward the end of the second trimester or at twenty-four weeks gestation. And reports of earlier survivals are rare but true. In the near future, medical advancements may make this age earlier. Present-day ultrasound can pick up a pregnancy by seven weeks gestation.

The term *therapeutic abortion* is often used for any voluntary interruption of pregnancy. The true medical definition of a therapeutic abortion, however, is the intervention in and termination of a pregnancy when the mother's life or health is significantly at risk by allowing the pregnancy to continue.[7]

TYPES OF ABORTION

The method of abortion used depends on the physician's preference or the type necessary due to the age of the fetus (see table 1). A brief description of each procedure follows.

Suction Curettage

Suction curettage, also called vacuum aspiration, is the most frequent type of abortion done in the first twelve weeks of pregnancy (93 percent of first-trimester abortions).[8] The day before the scheduled abortion, the woman's cervix is

Table 1
TYPES OF ABORTION

Abortion Type	Gestation Age	Percent of All Abortions Performed
Suction curettage	1 to 12 wks.	95%
Dilatation and evacuation	12 to 24 wks.	1.8%
Saline	16 to 24 wks.	3.1%
Hysterotomy	26 wks. to term	0.06%
Menstrual extraction		
Pharmaceutical agents		
RU-486		
Prostaglandin E2		
Cytotec		

usually dilated with *Laminaria* (a Japanese seaweed) or similar synthetic product. The long, thin, tubular dehydrated seaweed is inserted into the cervical canal. As the *Laminaria* absorbs the cervical moisture, it swells, dilating the cervix. This gradual dilatation causes less cervical trauma than using instruments.

After twenty-four hours the cervix is dilated enough to allow a long, hollow plastic tube with a sharp beveled edge into the uterus. Suction is connected to the other end of the tube. As the sharp edge breaks up the fetus, the fetal parts are suctioned into a collecting jar. Observers can see recognizable human parts if the fetus is ten weeks or older. If the fetus is too large to be totally suctioned out by this method, the suction is turned off and the uterus is manually scraped out (curettage) to assure that the abortion is complete.

Dilatation and Evacuation (D&E)

This is the most common method of terminating a pregnancy in the second trimester (between sixteen and twenty weeks). Again the dilatation is done by inserting *Laminaria* into the cervical canal the day before the scheduled abortion. The next day the *Laminaria* is removed, and the membranes are ruptured with a sharp instrument. The fetus is broken up inside the uterus and withdrawn in pieces with forceps. The uterus is curetted at the end of the procedure to make sure that the placenta has also separated from the uterus.

Saline Abortion

Saline (salt water) is injected into the uterus through the abdominal wall after the same amount of amniotic fluid has been withdrawn. This technique is usually done in the second trimester of pregnancy. The fetus swallows the saline, and the high-salt concentration "poisons" the fetus. The saline environment and the death of the fetus induce uterine contractions. The dead fetus is usually delivered intact twelve to forty-eight hours after the initial injection of saline.

Hysterotomy

This is essentially a Caesarean section. The uterus is opened abdominally; the fetus is delivered and left to die.

Menstrual Extraction

Popular in the early 1970s, before abortion was legal, menstrual extraction (ME) is still being used today as a home remedy for undesired pregnancies, despite available opportunities for more sterile medical procedures. A four-millimeter plastic tube is inserted into the undilated cervix (usually by a friend of the pregnant woman), and a plastic syringe is pumped to create suction and withdraw the uterine contents. The procedure takes between ten to thirty minutes and is performed up to the eighth week of gestation.[9] Pamphlets and videotapes demonstrating how to do the procedure are available from the Federation of Feminist Women's Health Centers. This method is used regularly in other countries including Mexico, where abortion is illegal. The American College of Obstetricians and Gynecologists (ACOG) recommends that the procedure be done only by a physician.

Pharmaceutical Agents

RU-486, used since 1982, is the latest and most controversial abortion-producing drug produced by pharmaceutical companies. Presently available in France and China, this hormone (mifepristone) is reported to be very effective in bringing about an abortion early in pregnancy.

How does it work? RU-486 antagonizes progesterone (a hormone manufactured by the ovary), which is needed to prepare the uterus for implantation of a fertilized egg. When RU-486 is taken orally within forty-two days of the last menstrual period, it can terminate pregnancy in 80 percent of the attempts. The percentage can be increased to 95 percent as many as forty-nine days after the last menstrual period if the woman receives a prostaglandin treatment (vaginally or by injection) thirty-six to forty-eight hours after taking the RU-486.[10]

This treatment flushes out the fertilized egg by inducing vaginal bleeding within one to three days. The bleeding usually lasts ten to eleven days and is heavier than a normal menstrual period.[11]

Potential side effects (when used with the progesterone) include nausea, vomiting, diarrhea, and excessive blood loss requiring blood transfusions.[12] Another 10 percent of the women require narcotics to control the pain.

Prostaglandin E2 is a vaginal gel presently used to soften and dilate the cervix and induce labor. It can be used to abort pregnancies from the thirteenth week on. Babies aborted in this manner are often born alive but left to die.

Cytotec is a drug manufactured for use in patients with stomach ulcers from arthritis medications. It causes abortions in women who become pregnant while on the drug.

COMPLICATIONS AT THE TIME OF ABORTION

Women can experience complications of abortions not only at the time of the abortions but also in future pregnancies. Complications from abortions can be divided into several categories (see tables 2 and 3). These complications are well documented even in pro-abortion literature. Speculation exists as to whether these complications are still less than can be anticipated if the woman allowed the pregnancy to proceed. Pregnancy itself is certainly not free of complications. However, most physicians would concur that any artificial intervention in a person's health (including pregnancy) leads to more problems than allowing nature "to take its course." One of the first things physicians learn in medical school is *Primum non Nocere:* First, do no harm.

What are some of the complications surrounding abortions?

Table 2
COMPLICATIONS AT THE TIME OF ABORTION

Infection
     endometritis
     PID
Bleeding (hemorrhage)
     uterine perforation
     uterine atony

DIC
retained products of conception
Bowel laceration
Bladder laceration
Damage to cervix
  tears
  bleeding
Missed ectopic pregnancy
Anesthesia complications
Death

Infections

Infections as a result of an elective abortion have been reported in up to 30 percent of all abortions.[13]

Endometritis (infection of the uterine lining) occurs in 5 percent of all abortions.[14] Younger women are affected twice as often as older women.[15]

Pelvic Inflammatory Disease (PID) is the most significant infectious complication. Causing infection in the fallopian tubes, PID can lead to infertility and an increased incidence of ectopic (tubal) pregnancy.[16] After one episode of PID, there is a 12.8 percent frequency of sterility. That figure increases to 35.5 percent after two or more bouts of PID.[17] Women who experience multiple episodes of PID are extremely susceptible to recurrent pelvic pain, menstrual pain, and painful intercourse.[18]

Chlamydia infections at the time of the abortion place women at high risk. If the woman has chlamydia in the cervix at the time of the abortion, the risk of PID after the abortion increases from 10 percent to 28 percent.[19] Chlamydia is the most prevalent sexually transmitted disease (STD), and every woman should be tested for it prior to any abortion. Despite this, a report from the busiest abortion clinic in Minneapolis reported culturing women only for gonorrhea and not for chlamydia.

Many abortionists give the woman enough antibiotics for four days following the abortion. This may prevent infection obtained at the time of the abortion, but it is not a full treatment regimen for a chlamydia infection. Women then come to emergency rooms or to their own physicians one to two months after the abortion with a full-blown PID that should have been picked up at the time of the abortion but subsequently spread to the fallopian tubes. These infections are very rarely included as actual complications of abortion.

Bleeding

Bleeding (hemorrhaging) is a major complication following induced abortion.

Uterine Perforation is the most severe cause of bleeding following an abortion. If the abortionist suspects a perforation, the abortion should be immediately stopped, and no further intrauterine manipulation should be allowed, even if the abortion was not completed. If the bleeding can't be stopped, abdominal surgery may be necessary to look at the damaged uterus. Some perforations are severe enough that a hysterectomy is needed to stop the bleeding. For every two-week increase in the gestational age of the fetus, the risk of uterine perforation increases 1.4 times.[20]

Uterine Atony is when the uterus sometimes will not contract immediately after the abortion, and significant bleeding will occur until appropriate medications are given. Severe bleeding may lead to a total loss of clotting factors in the blood, a condition called Disseminated Intravascular Coagulation (*DIC*). This is a true obstetrical emergency, often requiling immediate blood transfusions and possibly an emergency hysterectomy.

Retained Products of Conception sometimes remain imbedded in the uterus and continue to bleed until they are removed by a repeat curettage. In the premature interruption of the pregnancy, the placenta is not as likely to release from the uterine wall. This can cause significant bleeding and other complications.

Bowel and Bladder Perforation

Some uterine perforations are also associated with lacerations to the bowel and bladder. Damaging either of these results in "spillage" of their contents into the abdomen, requiring immediate surgery.

Damage to the Cervix

Cervical damage can occur in several ways during an abortion. The main problem is tears caused by aggressive dilatation, which precipitates severe bleeding and later scarring. Women who have not previously delivered a baby are at twice the risk for cervical damage since their cervix has never been stretched before.[21] Cervical tears occur in 57 percent of women who have not previously delivered a live infant.[22]

Missed Ectopic Pregnancies

Ectopic pregnancies include all pregnancies in which fertilized eggs embed themselves in tissue outside the uterus (most often in the fallopian tubes). These situations can be missed in early pregnancy, and if the abortion is performed as if the fetus is in the uterus, the ectopic pregnancy may go undetected until the tube ruptures, requiring emergency surgery. The woman faces increased risk of complications, future fertility problems, and even death. The woman often doesn't report the pain of the ectopic pregnancy because she thinks it is normal after an abortion. Identification of the fetus and its location at the time of the abortion is mandatory to prevent these complications. However, abortionists do not always obtain pathology specimens.

Uterine Anomalies

Abnormalities in the uterus make it difficult to diagnose pregnancies and subsequently perform abortions. Sometimes a uterus is heart shaped, and the abortionist suctions out the wrong half of the uterus, leaving the pregnancy in place. This creates the need for more tests, another procedure, and further psychological trauma for the patient.

Anesthesia Complications

As in any type of surgical procedure, anesthesia complications are unavoidably present during abortions. General anesthesia during abortion increases blood loss, especially if medications that relax the uterus are used. The risk of death from anesthesia-related complications is two to four times greater with general anesthesia than with local or regional anesthesia.[23]

Death

Death is also a known complication of abortion. As noted at the beginning of this chapter, death statistics can't be accurately determined, and the figures we do have are difficult to interpret. Between 1974 and 1978, the Centers for Disease Control reported 141 abortion-related deaths—63 related to legal abortion.[24] Maternal mortality data showed 188 abortion-related deaths during the same time period—92 related to legal abortion.[25] These are almost as many deaths per year as occurred before *Roe* v. *Wade*. What is more frightening is the fact that illegal back-alley abortions are still happening when legal abortions are readily available.

COMPLICATIONS AFFECTING FUTURE PREGNANCIES

Not only do women face complications at the time of their abortion, but they also face complications in future pregnancies.

Table 3
COMPLICATIONS AFFECTING FUTURE PREGNANCIES

Infertility
Bleeding
Ectopic pregnancy
Placenta previa
Subsequent miscarriages
Fetal malpresentations
Premature births and early infant death
Cervical stenosis
Cervical incompetence

Infertility

Studies show that infertility is a problem that occurs after 3 percent to 5 percent of all abortions.[26]

Bleeding

Women who have had one or more abortions are more likely to have bleeding in the first three months of a subsequent pregnancy.

Ectopic Pregnancy

The risk of ectopic (tubal) pregnancy doubles for women after one abortion and can be as high as four times greater for women who have had two or more previous abortions.[27] This risk is believed to be most related to the incidence of PID.

Placenta Previa

Placenta previa, a condition in which the placenta is implanted abnormally low in the uterus, has been found to be a seven-to-fifteen times greater risk in women who have had abortions.[28] Some experts speculate that because of excessive trauma to the lining of the uterus during a previous abortion, in subsequent pregnancies the placenta lodges in the lower segment of the uterus, the segment that was previously unaffected. Some of the possible complications of a placenta previa include bleeding during pregnancy or labor, a need for a Caesarean section, placental separation, and miscarriage.

Subsequent Miscarriages

Multiple studies indicate that women who have had abortions are twice as likely to experience subsequent miscarriages. The figure is tripled if the woman has had two or more abortions. And these statistics were collected after abortion was legalized. They are not explained by other risk factors.[29] Cervical incompetence is a contributing factor, however.

Fetal Malpresentations

After having one abortion, a woman who again becomes pregnant is more likely to find that the baby's birth position will be unusual. Obstetricians report an excess of number of malpresentations (both breech and transverse lie—lying crosswise in the womb) in women who have had abortions.[30]

Premature Births and Early Infant Death

According to several studies, premature births are more frequent in women who have had a previous abortion.[31] Early death in infants born after their mother had an abortion occurs two to four times more often than when the mother has never had an abortion.[32]

HYDATIDIFORM MOLES

While hydatidiform moles are a rare complication of pregnancy, they are worthy of discussion because abortions that are not verified pathologically as fetal tissue can actually be hydatidiform moles. These can be cancerous, and aggressive follow-up is needed. Hydatidiform moles can cause death if not adequately treated.

7

Emotional Effects of Abortion

Women and men who have had abortions experience a wide range of emotional symptoms. At first they may experience only relief that the crisis pregnancy has been terminated. Some may repress or deny their emotions and rationalize that they made the only decision they could under the circumstances. Others may deny for years that they are struggling with emotional stress.

Post-abortive women and men who are in denial or repression for years will not be healed with time; their psychological state will continue to deteriorate until they seek help. They will not be able to resolve these emotional problems until they identify and deal with them.

Some women and men seem to have more emotional symptoms than others. What makes the difference?

First, the moral code the women and men live by or learned in their family affects how they view the abortion experience. If their moral code tells them that taking life is wrong, they will struggle deeply with their abortion decision. Even if they don't think about it at the time, their convictions may impact them many years later when they face the fact that they have taken the life of their child.

Second, the abortion experience may have greater impact on women and men who felt forced or manipulated into the abortion. They may struggle with feelings of anger, distrust, and bitterness toward those who pressured them. Or if the mother of the unborn child had to make the decision alone, she may feel she has no one to blame but herself, leaving her with great emotional stress. On the other hand, if the father of the unborn child was left out of the decision-making process, he often feels angry, betrayed, and helpless.

Third, the abortion procedure itself and the trauma surrounding the experience may also significantly affect the woman. If she sees the baby or the baby's body parts, if she is held down and treated uncaringly, or if she suffers some other traumatic experience around the time of the abortion, she may experience severe emotional distress.

Based on the responses of the women who completed the Conquerors survey, this chapter will explore the various emotional symptoms they experienced as a result of their abortion experience: guilt and shame; grief-related emotions (denial, isolation, anger, bargaining, depression, acceptance); fear and anxiety; as well as obsessive, compulsive, and addictive behaviors. Because the Conquerors men did not participate in this study, the following discussion does not include their emotional symptoms. But as you read their stories in chapter 10, you will see many of the same emotional symptoms.

GUILT AND SHAME

A great deal of guilt and shame often haunt the abortion experience. As many as 90 percent of the women in the Conquerors study recognized guilt and shame feelings related to their abortion. It is important to realize, however, that guilt and shame are not the same.

Guilt is a God-given emotion that tells us when we have broken one of his commandments. *Shame* is an emotion that says we are defective people. Shame says not only that our deeds are bad but that we are bad people.

Guilt

Some professionals say that guilt is a product of the Christian faith. They assert that if the church didn't weigh down people with the commandments and other biblical directives, people wouldn't feel guilt. These professionals don't realize that God in his mercy and grace understood the sinful nature of women and men. He knew that the guilt they experienced when they sinned needed to be forgiven by a holy God so that they could receive emotional and spiritual healing.

One woman describes the guilt she has experienced: "I have always felt guilty about the abortion. It was the wrong thing to do. The child was the result of an affair I had. I had a rotten marriage and already had a young baby to care for. When I went to the doctor to talk to him about having an abortion, he did something to start the process and then scheduled a time for me to go to the hospital to abort the baby. When I got to the hospital, I panicked and said I didn't want to go through with it, but it was too late. To this day I feel guilty. I have had a hard time forgiving myself."

The guilt that this woman feels is natural, but she needs to learn to accept God's forgiveness (see step 7 in chapter 17).

Shame

Many survey participants indicated they had been brought up in families that gave them shaming messages about who they are as people. These messages were expressed directly or implied through facial expressions or failure to acknowledge a job well done. The women had been told that they were dumb or stupid or the worst kid there ever was. They often were compared to their siblings, making them feel as if they never measured up and never did anything right.

The woman who has had an abortion may continue to give these shaming messages *to herself.* She may think that she is an evil, terrible woman whom God does not care about and whom he could never forgive. Because she is unable to accept God's forgiveness, she often becomes perfectionistic, trying to buy approval from God and others in an attempt to compensate for the loss of her child. She tries to meet her needs and find her self-esteem through things and others (see step 3 in chapter 13).

GRIEF-RELATED EMOTIONS

When a woman goes through an abortion, she experiences grief at the death of her child. The stages of her grief parallel the stages outlined by Elisabeth Kubler-Ross in her book *On Death and Dying:* denial, isolation, anger, bargaining, depression, and acceptance.[1] The grief process following an abortion may be equally or more difficult than grieving the loss of a child who dies from natural causes. Why?

First, a woman has great difficulty grieving the loss of an aborted child, whom she has never seen, held, named, or acknowledged as living. She has held no formal grieving service like a funeral, where she can openly acknowledge the death of her child. She may continually think about the aborted child, wondering if it was a girl or a boy, what it looked like, and what kind of personality it had. In the Conquerors study, 50 percent of the women were preoccupied with thoughts about the aborted baby, and 51.5 percent had flashbacks of the aborted baby at unexpected times.

Second, our culture doesn't recognize the aborted fetus as a child and doesn't give the woman permission to grieve the death of that child as she would another child who had died. She may not have told her loved ones about the abortion for fear of rejection, so she must grieve alone or with others who feel uncomfortable with her grief and do not offer support.

Third, the woman's decision to take the life of her own child may fill her with guilt and shame. This will inhibit her grief process. Because she views abortion as self-inflicted, she denies her feelings of loss and replaces them with guilt and shame. She begins a vicious dialogue with herself:

"Oh, I feel so empty!"

"Yes, but you did it to yourself. You deserve this pain."

"You're right. I should just try to forget it."

Fourth, the post-abortive woman does not have *time* to grieve. She must get back to school or to her job. She must pretend all is well even though she has gone through a traumatic experience.

Finally, only a few counselors are trained to recognize or counsel a woman with post-abortion symptoms. This makes it difficult for a woman to get the help she needs.

The post-abortive woman herself may not understand that she is going through a grieving stage because she may be repressing her feelings of loss. She may be denying what is going on around her.

Denial

The stage for denial is set when the woman enters the abortion clinic or hospital. The nurses and doctors often say that the baby is a "mass of tissue," denying that the woman is aborting a child. The abortion personnel perpetuate this denial by not providing an opportunity for the woman to share her feelings (fear, sadness, anger) before, during, or after the abortion procedure. Nurses and doctors discourage any crying, strong expression of anger, or discussion about taking the life of a baby. The woman is hushed and told "everything will be okay." Dealing with the reality of the woman's trauma could make other patients and medical personnel uncomfortable.

One young woman describes how she denied the reality of what was happening to her: "I was raised to respect doctors and nurses, and I somehow thought they knew best. It confused me when abortion was presented as an okay thing to do. I started thinking that maybe I was wrong or that because they are knowledgeable, abortion is all right." The medical personnel helped perpetuate her denial.

The denial continues as the woman goes home. The few people who know she has had an abortion feel uncomfortable talking about it. The woman wants to repress and deny her uncomfortable feelings and get on with her life. But repression and denial lead to feelings of isolation.

Isolation

In the Conquerors study, 74 percent of the women admitted feelings of isolation. Because of the shame and secrecy surrounding the abortion, many women feel alone and misunderstood. They often agonize over their abortion decision for weeks. Those who give input may not be supportive of the woman's true feelings. This, too, causes isolation and alienation.

If the woman is part of the Christian community or if her family's moral code condemns abortion, the woman may feel isolated from her support system and also from God. If she is not able to reconcile her relationship to God, her grief may cause even greater isolation and hopelessness.

Anger

After an abortion a woman often uses anger as a defense mechanism to protect herself from her true feelings of sadness, guilt, and shame. In the Conquerors study, 82 percent of the women were able to identify anger they felt toward themselves for the crisis pregnancy, the abortion, or subsequent behavior.

As many as 60 percent recognized anger toward others. One woman explains it this way: "When I came out of denial, I was very angry. I was angry because my boyfriend didn't try to stop me. I was angry because the abortion clinic didn't give me decent counseling or provide me with alternatives. I was even angry with people around me who didn't notice I was suffering and didn't understand what I was going through."

Many women expressed anger toward the baby's father or toward men in general. This may cause extremes in sexual behavior. The Conquerors study shows that 24 percent of the women were more fearful of sexual intercourse after the abortion experience. Angry with the men who got them pregnant and/or angry with themselves over the crisis pregnancy and subsequent abortion, they feared getting pregnant again.

A post-abortive woman also may find herself angry with pregnant women. She may be angry that others have their babies when she has aborted hers. In the Conquerors study, 31 percent said they tried to avoid pregnant women. Often this is the result of their grief over the loss of their own child. In 4 percent of the responses, the women's anger was so strong that they acknowledged a desire for other women to abort their babies, feeling that if others aborted, it would somehow justify their own abortion.

A post-abortive woman also may find herself angry with children. In our study, 21 percent admitted feeling angry just seeing other babies or children.

When post-abortive women recognize their anger, they take the first step toward healing and forgiveness. "I was angry at others because I was angry with myself. Until I had forgiven myself, I could not forgive anyone else. I became critical and judgmental—truly an angry victim. After accepting God's forgiveness, I was able to freely forgive others. I now have compassion and understanding that I never had before. The Lord is bringing out of the ashes something good. This great weakness has become my strength." Chapters 12 and 17 deal more extensively with anger and forgiveness.

Bargaining

In the process of grieving the loss of her child through abortion, a woman may start to bargain with herself or with God. First, she may get pregnant again to produce a "replacement child," giving this child all the time, energy, and worldly goods she can supply. This woman is somehow trying to compensate for aborting the life of one child by responding excessively to every need of the replacement child. In the Conquerors survey, 53 percent of the women acknowledged that after their abortion experience, they desired to get pregnant again to compensate for their loss.

Different women handle replacement pregnancies different. Janice, a twenty-year-old Christian woman who had been pressured into an abortion, filled her loss by getting pregnant again within a year. Having given another child life, Janice felt she had paid her debt, and she gave this baby up for adoption.

Barb, a pregnant Christian woman in her late teens, felt compelled to keep her baby. When the pregnancy counselor questioned what had happened to make her so desperate to keep her child, Barb broke down and cried. She admitted that she had had an abortion less than a year before without telling anyone, and she now *had* to keep this baby to make up for taking the life of her first child.

Post-abortive women bargain or try to make amends for their abortion in a second way by becoming active in the pro-life movement or a crisis pregnancy ministry. If the post-abortive woman has dealt with her own grief, these activities can be therapeutic, and she can have an effective ministry because she understands what these women are going through. But if she has not dealt with her grief, she is only trying to make up for what she has done.

In her book *Helping Women Recover from Abortion*, Nancy Michels talks about the post-abortive woman who becomes an active speaker for pro-life causes: "She rationalizes that she is helping women by providing them with the facts of abortion, but inside she believes that she is making up or 'paying her dues' for the abortion she has had. 'If I speak enough times,' she thinks, 'then that will make up for my abortion—it will help erase what I've done.'"[2]

Depression

Depression is common in women who have had abortions. In the Conquerors study, 76 percent of the women stated that they had suffered or were suffering from depression. Although post-partum depression often follows childbirth, miscarriages, still birth, and abortions, many post-abortive women experience depression many years after their abortion because they have denied and repressed their feelings of guilt, shame, anger, and loss.

A woman may not see the connection between this depression and the loss she is experiencing from the abortion. Because she avoids getting in touch with her feelings, she may feel sad without knowing why. In the Conquerors study, 88 percent of the women acknowledged struggling with feelings of sadness.

Another way depression can manifest itself is through self-pity. The Conquerors study revealed that 50 percent of the women admitted they struggled with self-pity. A woman may question, "Why did this happen to me?" She often sits around, feeling sorry for herself and blaming others for not understanding her.

When a woman is depressed, her self-esteem suffers. In the Conquerors study, 78 percent of the women said they struggled with low self-esteem. The emotional trauma of an abortion is difficult for a woman whose self-esteem is intact, but the abortion experience may heap even greater feelings of inadequacy on a woman who has struggled with feelings of inferiority in the past. The guilt, shame, and grief that have plagued her life loom larger. She may feel she can't handle even everyday situations.

In cases of severe depression the woman feels a sense of hopelessness, futility, and inability to enjoy simple pleasures like eating, relationships, or nature. In the Conquerors study, 57 percent of the women identified a feeling of despair and hopelessness in their lives.

Again, each woman may react in a number of ways. Some feel out of control (71 percent), overemotional (68 percent), confused (63 percent), or unable to express emotions at all (56 percent). Many do not understand what is happening to them or why they feel the way they do. Unable to predict when intense crying spells will erupt, they feel out of control. As they become more depressed, they may feel numb, confused, unable to express any feelings at all.

Depression also affects sleep patterns. According to the Conquerors study, 25 percent of the post-abortive women suffered from insomnia. Although they may be very tired, they can't drop off to sleep or may sleep fitfully, struggling with their emotions, replaying what could have been or worrying about the future. One woman in the survey admitted, "I'm currently battling frequent nightmares about harming myself and my children. After the abortion, I had nightmares in which I would see the aborted baby dressed in black and trying to haunt me." Another 47 percent of the survey respondents indicated an excessive desire to sleep. Feeling unable to face people and responsibilities, these women want to stay in bed much of the time.

Sometimes a depressed woman experiences a loss of appetite. Their senses become dulled and food doesn't even look good. It takes great effort to eat small portions. If this behavior would continue, they could become weak, listless, and malnourished. The Conquerors study revealed 29 percent of the women had significantly decreased appetites after their abortion.

A woman who is depressed usually is not interested in sexual activity either. If a husband doesn't understand that his wife is depressed, he may take her refusals as rejection of him. This would only heap more shame on her for not meeting his needs.

But as a woman's depression deepens, she feels unable to help herself or receive help from anyone else, even God. Many post-abortive women entertain thoughts of suicide, and a few attempt it. In psychologist Dr. Vincent Rue's study of post-abortive women, 12 percent admitted having suicidal thoughts, and 3 percent had attempted suicide.[3] He also stated that women who were psychiatric patients before they had their abortions were three times more likely to need therapy after an abortion. Many people who promote abortions say it is better for an emotionally unstable young woman to abort her baby than to bring the baby to term. But Dr. Rue's findings seem to indicate that it would be far more traumatic for a troubled young woman to go through the abortion procedure.

A few years ago Tanya, a pregnant, emotionally unstable Christian woman I knew, was hospitalized for chemical dependency. Medical personnel and counselors strongly advised her to have an abortion. Tanya knew it wasn't right and told them she didn't want one, but they kept pressuring her day after day until she gave in. On the night of the abortion Tanya was overcome with guilt. She broke a drinking glass and slit her wrist. The staff had to lock her up in a psychiatric unit to prevent her from taking her life.

The Conquerors study revealed much higher percentages of suicidal thoughts and attempts than the percentages resulting from other studies. In the Conquerors study, 41 percent reported suicidal thoughts and 10 percent had attempted suicide. Since so many of the women in our study come from Christian or at least religious backgrounds, we could speculate that their religious value system gives them a conscience more sensitive to the guilt of their sin. And when this is not resolved, they have stronger feelings of hopelessness.

Sometimes a post-abortive woman wants to commit suicide because she feels she is such a bad person that the world would be better off without her. Though she may be afraid she will go to hell, she feels she deserves it. And even though a woman is a Christian, she may have lost hope that God cares whether she lives or dies. If she feels she will still go to heaven, she may rationalize that if she dies, she will be with her child.

Acceptance

The final stage of grief for the post-abortive woman is acceptance. When a woman reaches this point, she can fully acknowledge that she has lost a child—permanently. She can't bring the child back, and no other child can ever replace the child lost through abortion.

Even after a post-abortive woman has worked through the stages of denial, isolation, anger, bargaining, and depression, she may still experience feelings of sadness and remorse when she thinks about the child. Particularly painful times include the anniversary of the abortion or other important dates related to the abortion experience. These times of grief are normal if they are not prolonged.

FEAR AND ANXIETY

Post-abortive women are often filled with fear and anxiety. Some of their greatest fears include disclosure, intimacy, medical personnel, God's punishment, and infertility. Both the Conquerors study and Anne Speckhard's study reveal the range of anxiety post-abortive women experience.[4]

Dr. Speckhard says that in addition to fearing that others would find out about the abortion, the women in her study showed an increased distrust of men—primarily men who were potential or actual sex partners.[5] Comments from the Conquerors study support this view: "Because of the abortion I'm fearful of emotional intimacy, fearful of having another destructive-type relationship to a man, and fearful of being rejected if I don't allow myself to be sexually active."

Speckhard also indicated that post-abortive women fear doctors and health providers. Many women felt that medical personnel had lied to them about the details of the abortion, and many avoided seeing a doctor for some time afterward because of this lack of trust.[6] One of the Conquerors study participants commented: "Since I've had the abortion, I feel afraid when I have to fill out medical forms for physicals. I've never marked the box indicating that I've had an abortion. I don't trust people to be understanding, and I know if I were asked about it, I would burst into tears."

ANXIETY IN POST-ABORTIVE WOMEN

Conquerors Study		Speckhard Study	
Anxiety in general	79%	Fear that others will learn of abortion	89%
Nervousness	66%	Distrust of men	58%
Fear of medical exams	41%	Feelings of anxiety	54%
Fear of sexual intercourse	37%	Distrust of others	50%
Fear of the future	32%	Fear of retributive God	50%
Fear of medical personnel	24%	Fear of future infertility	46%
Fear of people	22%		
Fear of sounds of abortion	21%		
Fear of crowds	16%		
Non-specific fears	24%		

Speckhard found that women's fear of infertility directly correlates to their fear that God would punish them because they had aborted their babies. Many women also feared that their reproductive organs may be damaged because of the abortion, prohibiting them from having other children. Any subsequent difficulties these women had in getting pregnant, they blamed on their abortion.

The women in the Conquerors study also expressed their fear and anxiety about how their abortions would affect other areas of their lives.

- "I had another daughter after my abortion, and when she was young, I was very fearful that she would be stolen from me. Now that she is ten, this feeling is not as intense, but sometimes I still get scared that she'll go somewhere and something awful will happen to her and she won't return home."

- "I have a great fear that I won't have any other children—that the baby I aborted was my only chance."

- "I'm fearful of the equipment noise at the dentist's office. It reminds me of the suction machine that was used to perform the abortion."

OBSESSIVE, COMPULSIVE, AND ADDICTIVE BEHAVIORS

If a post-abortive woman's fears and anxieties remain unresolved, she often develops behavior disorders. Her obsessive, compulsive, and/or addictive behavior may express itself in eating disorders or abuse of alcohol and drugs.

Eating Disorders

In the Conquerors study, 8.8 percent of the women identified themselves as having suffered from eating disorders (bulimia and anorexia). Of these women, 66.7 percent had increased problems with their eating disorder after their abortion.

Another 51.5 percent indicated they had problems with overeating and 23.5 expressed problems of undereating. The overeating behavior increased 54.3 percent, and the undereating behavior increased 50.1 percent after their abortion experience.

Other women suffered a loss of appetite (29.4 percent), and 65 percent of these women experienced a loss of appetite after their abortion experience. It's difficult to evaluate how many of the women who overeat, undereat, and suffer with a loss of appetite would fit into the eating-disorder category.

The differentiation between a person with an eating disorder and a person who just overeats is the quantity and combinations of the traits Linda Riebel and Jane Kaplan write about in their book, *Someone You Love Is Obsessed With Food:* "To the person with an eating conflict, food serves dozens of additional functions. . . . a consolation, a reward, an anesthetic, a procrastination device, a way to comply (accepting offered food), a punishment (I don't deserve to feel good about myself), a way of showing love, a means of expressing creativity, a diversion in times of boredom."[7]

Riebel and Kaplan also discuss three types of eating behaviors: "*Overeating* can consist of: nibbling all day, . . . consuming excessively large meals, or binging [as in bulimia]. *Purging* is the practice of trying to escape the consequences of overeating by getting rid of food, either by vomiting or by using laxatives or diuretics. . . . *Restricting* means eating less than the person needs, such as in severe dieting or anorexia."[8]

If food controls the post-abortive woman's life, causing relentless dieting to the point of emaciation; if she can't stop eating; or if she regularly purges the food she has eaten, she has a food disorder. If a post-abortive woman is struggling with overeating, she may be trying to protect herself from getting close to men or even other women. Food may be her means of dealing with guilt, anxiety, anger, and every other problem she has.

Alcohol and Drug Abuse

A significant number of women who participated in the Conquerors study acknowledged struggling with the use of alcohol and drugs: 37 percent of the women frequently used alcohol, and 21 percent frequently used drugs. Of the women who used alcohol, 48 percent began drinking after the abortion experience. Of the women who used drugs, 42.9 percent started using them after their abortion experience.

Alcohol and drugs are mood-altering chemicals. They affect a person's moods. After people have had a few drinks, they may feel they are able to be themselves or be more readily accepted by others.

Jeff Van Vonderen, a pastor who is a certified, chemical-dependency counselor, states: "Abuse is any use of a chemical substance that causes the user to become or act in a way that is other than normal for him. If a person with a mellow temperament becomes mean after using, that is abuse. If a person is normally cranky and uses a chemical to become pleasant, that is abuse."[9]

Some post-abortive women and men become physically or emotionally addicted to drugs and/or alcohol. Van Vonderen states that "physical addiction occurs when the cells of the body change the way they function because of the frequent use of certain chemical substances. The cells become accustomed to the presence of those substances."[10] Van Vonderen goes on to say that people can be emotionally dependent without being physically dependent. Emotional dependency happens when chemicals are used as a means to solve problems or to meet emotional needs.

When post-abortive women seek to meet their emotional needs and dull their abortion-related emotional pain through the use of chemicals, they risk becoming emotionally dependent on them. Van Vonderen tells how chemicals get in the way of God's plan for meeting their emotional needs: "If we turn to families and the body of Christ and they function as God intended, we are supported, our needs are met, and the need for chemical use seems ludicrous. However, if we turn to these resources and they do not do what God intended, or if we turn long enough to chemicals instead to meet our psycho/emotional needs, we will eventually lose our relationships. Then the need for further chemical use is reinforced."[11]

8

Spiritual Effects of Abortion

The emotional aftereffects of an abortion will have a profound influence on the spiritual struggles of post-abortive women and men. Past emotional wounds will deeply affect not only their concept of God but also their perception of the church. Many post-abortive women and men struggle with feelings of alienation, anger, guilt, and the inability to feel forgiven.

SPIRITUAL EFFECTS OF EMOTIONAL WOUNDS

Women and men who have emotional wounds usually exhibit feelings of inferiority and low self-esteem. When they become Christians and surrender their lives to the Lord, the old messages of low self-esteem get mixed up with how they think God sees them. They question how God could ever love them because they feel they are such bad people. David Seamands, professor of pastoral ministries at Asbury Theological Seminary, says that "the good news of the Gospel has not penetrated down into [their] damaged inner self, which also needs to be evangelized. [Their] deep inner scars must be touched and healed by the Balm of Gilead."[1]

Many post-abortive women and men who have a personal relationship to Jesus Christ are not able to receive his love, acceptance, and forgiveness. They continue in bondage to their low self-esteem, self-condemnation, and fears.

Many Christians, including pastors, mistakenly believe that when people become Christians or are filled with the Spirit, all their emotional problems evaporate. David Seamands disagrees, "This just isn't true. A great crisis experience of Jesus Christ, as important and eternally valuable as this is, is not a shortcut to emotional health. It is not a quickie cure for personality problems."[2]

Why is this so important to understand? Seamands explains,

> First of all, [we must understand this] so that we can compassionately live with ourselves and allow the Holy Spirit to work with special healing in our own hurts and confusions. We also need to understand this in order not to judge other people too harshly, but to have patience with their confusing and contradictory behavior. In so doing, we will be kept from unfairly criticizing and judging fellow Christians. They're not fakes, phonies, or hypocrites. They are people, like you and me, with hurts and scars and wrong programming that interfere with their present behavior.[3]

Seamands is not lowering the standards for Christians with emotional problems or denying the power of the Holy Spirit to heal emotional hangups. He believes that certain problems need special understanding, "an unlearning of past wrong programming, and a relearning and reprogramming transformation by the renewal of our minds."[4] This process of relearning, reprogramming, and renewing of one's mind takes time.

The apostle Paul knew that we can easily be "programmed" by the world's philosophy, and we need to reprogram our minds to follow God's ways. That's why he reminds us: "Do not conform any longer to the pattern of this world, but be transformed by the renewing of your mind" (Rom. 12:2). J. B. Phillips paraphrases the thought this way: "Don't let the world around you squeeze you into its own mold, but let God remold your minds from within, so that you may prove in practice that the plan of God for you is good, meets all his demands and moves toward the goal of true maturity."

VIEW OF GOD

As we look at the spiritual damage in women and men who have had an abortion experience, we need to keep in mind these questions: How do post-abortive women and men view God? Do they see him only as the Judge who waits to zap them whenever they do something wrong? Do they think that God is unable or unwilling to forgive them for the abortion? Do they see God as weak, uncaring, and uninvolved?

Many post-abortive women and men have a distorted image of God. They see him as the Old Testament God: holy and sometimes angry and vengeful. While these images of God are true, they are incomplete. The Old Testament also reminds us that God is "compassionate and gracious, slow to anger, abounding in love. . . . He does not treat us as our sins deserve" (Ps. 103:8–10).

And the New Testament also speaks of God's grace, mercy, forgiveness, and love. For instance, James 1:17 tells us that "Every good and perfect gift is from above, coming down from the Father of the heavenly lights, who does not change like shifting shadows."

ALIENATION

Sin brings alienation. The apostle Paul explains how this happens: "Their moral understanding is darkened and their reasoning is beclouded. [They *are*] alienated (estranged, self-banished) from the life of God . . . because of the . . . willful blindness . . . that is deep-seated in them, due to . . . the insensitiveness of their moral nature" (Eph. 4:18 AMPLIFIED, emphasis added).

Alienation from God

Sin alienates us from God. The Conquerors study revealed that 49 percent of the women said they felt alienated from God. While many unmarried sexually active women and men have unwittingly bought the lies surrounding "sexual freedom," once they have gone through with an abortion, they often realize the alienation this sin brings.

Alienation can come either from never knowing God or from knowing God but straying from him. A person, especially a Christian, usually doesn't consciously decide to be sexually active. The path to sin is a subtle, step-by-step process. First, people allow their minds to dwell on the idea of sexual involvement; then they feel temptation. Next they give in to temptation. And the more they continue this pattern, the more enslaved they become. Their consciences become insensitive, and they hardly notice that they have become separated from God. If their sexual activity leads to an unwanted pregnancy, they may decide to abort. Taking the life of their unborn child simply alienates them further.

When they finally become aware of this alienation, they

are afraid God would never consider forgiving them. His love and acceptance do not feel real to them.

Alienation from the Church

Ashamed of their behavior and convinced that they deserve condemnation, post-abortive women and men also may feel that people in the church could not accept their sin or forgive them. Therefore, they separate themselves from the body of Christ at a time when they most need that support.

The Conquerors study indicated that 40 percent of the women felt alienated from the church. One woman shares her struggle with feelings of alienation: "I'm afraid that the church community will find out I had an abortion and will reject me. I also fear that a good Christian man won't want me."

Some post-abortive women and men overcome their fear enough to tell a pastor or layperson about the abortion and about their inability to accept God's forgiveness. If these Christians listen carefully to the guilt, shame, and remorse the post-abortive women and men feel and if these Christians can express their acceptance and forgiveness of the post-abortive women and men, then healing can begin. However, too often this kind of understanding does not take place. Instead, the post-abortive woman or man is told to read the Bible more, pray more, attend church more, or have more faith. These "solutions" only add more guilt and shame to women and men who have deep emotional wounds. Past wounds *hinder* them from trusting God, from praying, from believing the Scriptures, or from exercising their faith.

The church needs to demonstrate Christ's mercy and love to these women and men. Unless their emotional wounds are exposed to the healing touch of Jesus, they can't experience the abundant life Christ desires for all. The apostle Paul gives us this tremendous promise: "Once you were alienated from God and were enemies in your minds because of your evil behavior. But now he has reconciled you by Christ's physical body through death to present you holy in his sight, without blemish and free from accusation—if you continue in your faith, established and firm, not moved from the hope held out in the gospel" (Col. 1:21–23).

ANGER TOWARD GOD

Many post-abortive women and men feel angry with God. In the Conquerors study, 28 percent of the women admitted feeling anger toward God. Many feel that God will punish them for aborting their babies by making them infertile, making their other children die, or giving them a handicapped baby.

They are also angry with God because they feel that if he loved them, he would have protected them from the sins that entrapped them. It's important for post-abortive women and men to remember that God has given them a free will. James 1:13–15 says, "When tempted, no one should say, 'God is tempting me.' For God cannot be tempted by evil, nor does he tempt anyone; but each one is tempted when, by his own evil desire, he is dragged away and enticed. Then, after desire has conceived, it gives birth to sin; and sin, when it is full-grown, gives birth to death."

James clearly teaches that our own desires lure us into sin, but it is our choice. The end result is spiritual death. But the good news is that if we confess our sins to God, he will forgive us. "I acknowledged my sin to you and did not cover up my iniquity. I said, 'I will confess my transgressions to the Lord'—and you forgave the guilt of my sin" (Ps. 32:5).

Post-abortive women and men also may be angry with God because they feel they can't live up to his expectations.

They keep trying to please God by their good behavior. In their own strength they can't manifest the fruit of the Spirit, and they angrily blame God for their failure.

GUILT AND FORGIVENESS

Another spiritual issue post-abortive women and men struggle with is guilt and forgiveness. The Conquerors survey asked about guilt in two separate sections of the personal inventory. Guilt was listed under "Mental and Emotional Health" and under "Relationship to God." In the first category, 90 percent of the women admitted feelings of guilt, while in the latter category, 78 percent of the women checked "I struggle with guilt over my abortion experience." Why is there a discrepancy between the two guilt statistics? Perhaps the other 12 percent did not perceive their guilt as coming from God, or they feared identifying it as such.

Also, 62 percent admitted worrying about whether God would forgive them. The guilt and fear of not being forgiven is a heavy burden. The plight of these women is described in Psalm 32:3–4, "When I kept silent [about my sin], my bones wasted away through my groaning all day long. For day and night your hand was heavy upon me; my strength was sapped as in the heat of summer."

Many post-abortive women and men feel that even though they have confessed their sin and have asked God's forgiveness, they do not feel a release from the guilt. Commenting on this response, Dr. Anne Speckhard says, "The levels of denial and repression that exist in regard to the abortion frequently prevent [them] from confessing the abortion honestly and entirely, even to God. The horror of what [they have] done and [their] fears of facing it are so great that [they approach] reconciliation with God on a surface level only."[5] Speckhard goes on to say that when post-abortive women and men have sought the Lord in a less-than-honest manner, they will find no lasting peace or assurance of being forgiven. Instead, despair and frustration follow.

One of the women in the Conquerors study tells about her struggle with forgiveness: "I know that Jesus died for us so that we can be forgiven, but I still think daily about whether I really am forgiven. I just hope that God knows how I feel and that he will forgive me."

DRAWN CLOSER TO GOD

Although many people have found that their abortion experience has made them feel alienated from God, other people have found that their abortion experience drew them closer to God. The Conquerors survey revealed that 62 percent of the women felt closer to God as a result of their abortion experience. When the guilt and grief they experience becomes overwhelming, some women and men turn to the God of mercy, comfort, and forgiveness. One post-abortive man shared, "Had it not been for the abortion experience, I wonder if I would have my present relationship to Jesus Christ. Realizing this helps me overcome my painful experience."

The New Testament describes God as "the Father of compassion and the God of all comfort, who comforts us in all our troubles" (2 Cor. 1:3–4). The Lord is eager to help women and men in their healing process. He asks only for an attitude of humility and dependence on him. James says, "Humble yourselves before the Lord, and he will lift you up" (James 4:10).

Facing the truth about the abortion and being open to share that pain with God and others can be emotionally and spiritually freeing. In his book *With Open Hands,* theologian Henri J. M. Nouwen talks about the meaning of openness in prayer to God. "This openness . . . does not simply come of itself. It requires a confession that you are limited, dependent, weak, and even sinful. Whenever you pray, you profess that you are not God nor want to be God, that you haven't reached your goal yet, that you never will reach it in this life, that you must constantly stretch out your hands and wait for the gift of life. This attitude is difficult because it makes you vulnerable."[6]

Post-abortive women and men who want to find healing for their emotional wounds need to be vulnerable and open to God, honestly confessing their sin—including the abortion of their child. By turning their anger, alienation, and guilt over to God, they can find the love, comfort, forgiveness, and acceptance they desperately need.

Isaiah, prophesying about Jesus Christ, says: "He has sent me to bind up the brokenhearted, to proclaim freedom for the captives, . . . to comfort all who mourn, and provide for those who grieve . . . to bestow on them a crown of beauty instead of ashes, the oil of gladness instead of mourning, and a garment of praise instead of a spirit of despair. They will be called oaks of righteousness, a planting of the Lord for the display of his splendor" (Isa. 61:1–3).

PART III

Conquerors Post-Abortion
Support Program

9

What Is the Conquerors Program?

In all these things we are more than conquerors through him who loved us.
—Romans 8:37

In response to many requests for help in counseling women who have had abortions, New Life Family Services (NLFS) began to pray that God would establish a ministry to meet that need. He answered that prayer by sending two volunteers who had recovered from the damages their abortion experience had caused in their lives. Wanting to help women who were still struggling with unresolved issues after an abortion, these two women joined me, as NLFS director, in developing the Conquerors post-abortion support program in 1985.

Based on Romans 8:37: "In all these things we are more than conquerors through him who loved us," the Conquerors Nine-Steps-to-Recovery program provides a twelve-week program that helps participants conquer obstacles and pain through the power of God's love and through the loving care of a support group.

In 1989, men who had been involved in the abortion experience started coming to the Conquerors informational meetings to receive help. In 1990, the first Conquerors men's group was started using the Nine-Steps-to-Recovery format.

GROUP ORGANIZATION

The Conquerors support groups consist both of people who need help with their post-abortion experiences and of trained leaders, many of whom also have had an abortion experience. Ideally, for every eight participants, the group will provide one leader and one assistant leader.

Participants

Conquerors provides support groups for both women and men. Experience indicates that the groups are most effective when the two groups are separate—women's groups for women, men's groups for men.

Interview. All potential Conquerors group members must be interviewed. This interview is helpful for both the leader as well as the possible participant. The interview helps leaders assess the client's level of emotional stability. If the leader determines that the client could not handle the group sessions or would not benefit from the Conquerors support group at this particular time, the leader should make an appropriate referral to a professional counselor.

Agreement form. When women and men come to a Conquerors group, they are asked to make a commitment to certain criteria: regular attendance for the twelve-week period; completion of homework; payment of an affordable fee to cover the costs of the ministry.

Group Leaders

Group leaders facilitate the discussion in a group and guide the healing process. As we have said, ideally the group will provide two leaders for every eight participants so that the leaders can focus intensely on each participant, building stability and trust over the twelve-week period. The most important requirements for leaders are emotional stability and spiritual maturity.

Leadership training. If people who are not professional counselors wish to become group leaders, they must receive training and experience. The training helps potential leaders build their skills in interviewing, group development, active listening, use of confrontation, and handling difficult group members. Leaders also are trained to use the Conquerors manual and to handle post-abortion issues. See the bibliography for suggested reading for group leaders.

Supervision and consultation. If group leaders are not professional counselors, we recommend that a professional counselor or social worker be available to provide supervision, training, and consultation. Group leaders should meet regularly for support, consultation about difficult clients, and exchange of ideas about new information or methods.

Resources

Speakers. Conquerors groups invite Christian professionals (psychologists, counselors, social workers, pastors) and other qualified people to teach various aspects of the nine-step program.

Library. Many groups provide a resource library that includes books and materials to assist in the healing process (see bibliography for book list).

Personal story ringbinder. Most groups include in their resource library a ringbinder containing personal abortion stories, letters, and poems (appendix A & B) shared by group members (these do not need to be signed if the member wishes to remain anonymous). The ringbinder may also contain other writings, research, or articles that may be pertinent to post-abortion issues.

Meeting Format

Conquerors groups meet once a week for twelve consecutive weeks. Weekly meetings usually last two hours and include a large-group teaching session that follows the Nine-Steps-to-Recovery format (half hour to an hour), followed by small-group discussion that focuses on applying the teaching, homework questions, and assigned Scripture passages.

Goals. At the first meeting, group leaders explore what each woman or man would like to accomplish for herself or himself by the end of the twelve weeks. At the final meeting, group members re-examine these goals to assess individual progress and growth as well as evaluate the group experience.

Prayer. Prayer is important before, during, and after the Conquerors meetings. Leaders, individually and as a group, need to be grounded in prayer before each session. Prayer also can be part of each group meeting. It is appropriate to begin each meeting with prayer, asking God to guide and direct that session, and to close with prayer as well.

Confidentiality. It is essential if women and men are to open up and explore the full spectrum of their abortion experience. Many people find that they tell the support group things they have never before shared with anyone else. They must know from the outset that what they say as well as what they hear is not repeated outside of the group. Therefore, the ground rules of confidentiality must be established at the initial meeting.

CONTENT—NINE STEPS TO RECOVERY

The nine steps provide a progressive series of activities and issues that build on each other to bring healing and growth to post-abortive women and men.

Step 1— I recognize that I am powerless to heal the damage my abortion has caused in my life. I look to God for the power to make me whole.

Step 2— I will identify my feelings related to my abortion experience. I will start by exploring my feelings of fear and anxiety and my feelings of anger toward myself and others. I will acknowledge how these feelings have affected my life, and with God's help I will seek inner peace.

Step 3— I understand that the guilt, shame, and emotional distress I suffer may be consequences of my abortion. I will acknowledge these feelings and seek to resolve them.

Step 4— I will accept mourning as part of the healing process as I grieve the loss of my child. I will work through the stages of grief with the help of God.

Step 5— I am willing to confess to God that I am accountable for the loss of my child. I will honestly examine my own motives and actions as well as those of other people who were involved in my abortion decision.

Step 6— I will examine how my abortion experience has affected my past and present relationships. This will include the issues of communication, co-dependency, and sexuality.

Step 7— I accept responsibility for the loss of my aborted child, and I will accept God's forgiveness and choose to forgive myself and others.

Step 8— I acknowledge that I am a special person. I am important to God. With his help, I will develop a positive self-image and work toward my full potential.

Step 9— I acknowledge God's sovereignty and will strive to learn his plan for my life. I will choose to continue the process of healing from my abortion, and I will use my experience to encourage others and help bring restoration into their lives.[1]

10

Men in the Conquerors Program

Men play a significant role in the abortion experience, yet many people have neglected the special pain they bear as the result of this experience. Only recently have the needs of post-abortive men been recognized and addressed.

Since 1989, when New Life Family Services began its involvement with Conquerors men's groups, we have learned a great deal about the needs and feelings of post-abortive men. Basically the men's experiences fall into two categories: either their feelings and beliefs were not considered in the abortion decision or they were the ones who wanted the abortion.

MEN WHOSE BELIEFS WERE NOT CONSIDERED

Many men feel the anger and helplessness of not being allowed to have a voice in the abortion decision. Gary's story in chapter 1 describes the betrayal he felt because he was never even told about the first pregnancy and he was never consulted about the decision to abort his child. He felt devalued and unimportant.

Other men know about the pregnancy and object to an abortion, but their wives or girlfriends have an abortion anyway. The men feel helpless and angry toward a system that gives them no rights to safeguard the life of their unborn child. They want to protect the baby from being aborted and the woman they love from the abortion experience, but they can do neither. They become angry, not only toward the women but also toward themselves for not being able to prevent the situation. This anger turned inward often leads to depression, which further damages relationships and creates isolation.

Don Didn't Believe in Abortion

Don was a sensitive child raised in a strict Christian family that often condemned him, making him feel as if he couldn't do anything right. He hated going to church, and at the age of fifteen, he decided he didn't want to go anymore. But he did feel strongly about the sanctity of human life, and even as a young man he was opposed to abortion. He had determined in his heart that he would never take the life of his child.

As an adult, Don developed a tough façade to disguise his sensitivity and insecurity. After being very hurt by a close relationship to a woman, he kept his distance from women—until he met Pat.

Pat was married and had four children. Her love for her husband had died, and she wanted to end the marriage. Don and Pat secretly dated and soon developed a sexual relationship, which resulted in a pregnancy a few months later.

Pat's husband had had a vasectomy, so she felt she had no choice but to have an abortion. Don was deeply against abortion and encouraged Pat to leave her husband. He even promised to give her a large sum of money if she wouldn't abort the baby. But Pat felt abortion was the only solution. She even asked Don to pray for her and ask God to forgive her for aborting the baby.

When Don couldn't talk Pat out of having an abortion, he compromised his deepest convictions and took her to the abortion clinic. He rationalized that he loved her and wanted to help her, even to the point of paying for the abortion.

When they got to the abortion clinic, there were about thirty-five other women waiting to get an abortion. Don didn't say a word. When Pat went in for the procedure, he felt like screaming, but of course he didn't. When Pat came out of the recovery room, she was in complete denial, pretending that nothing had happened. Even Don felt somewhat relieved.

Two weeks later all the feelings about the abortion hit Don. Anger and hatred boiled inside him. Instead of yelling or talking it out with someone, he pushed it down. He had a hard time even talking to Pat. He felt he was carrying the pain and humiliation for both of them. He felt excruciating anguish. "It was hell," he says. "I thought I'd be better off dead." He became obsessed with the abortion, thinking about it day and night, often crying about it for hours. He became extremely anxious, even experiencing panic attacks.

Don tried to get out of the relationship. He still loved Pat and didn't want to be hateful to her, but it really bothered him that she would never admit that the abortion was wrong. She would just say, "I did what I had to do." He felt a lot of hatred toward her, himself, and the abortion experience.

When Don became a Christian some time later, he found some relief from the pain he was experiencing from the abortion. The Lord also softened his heart toward Pat, and he felt he should try to work out his relationship to her.

When Don sought pastoral counseling, the pastor told

him he needed to let go of Pat and go on with God. Don couldn't heed his advice at that time.

Pat got a divorce from her husband, and Don started seeing her a lot. Becoming pregnant a second time by Don, Pat reacted in rage. Over his strenuous objections, she had another abortion, which further destroyed their relationship.

Don is trying to get right with God again. Attending the Conquerors group for men has helped him in the abortion healing process. He realizes now his responsibility in the abortion experience and has asked God to forgive him. He has also forgiven Pat and is learning what constitutes a healthy relationship to a woman.

Joe Felt Helpless to Stop the Abortion

While Joe was dating Betty, she told him that she had had a child out of wedlock when she was younger. Her parents had pressured and shamed her into going away to a maternity home to place her child for adoption, fearing that if anyone found out about Betty's condition, their family would be crushed by the shame. Betty also told Joe that she had been sexually abused as a child, a reality her parents denied. Joe responded to this revelation with compassion and love. He found himself feeling very protective of Betty.

As their relationship deepened, they became sexually active, and within a year, Betty was pregnant for the second time. Worried about what her parents would say about the pregnancy, Betty asked Joe to go with her to tell them. Her mother screamed, "Why can't you control yourself?" Joe felt sad that Betty was so shamed and put down by her parents. Both sets of parents agreed that the best thing for Betty and Joe was to get married. The two started planning their wedding.

Suddenly Betty announced that she was going out of

state to have an abortion. Her parents again were pressuring her to make a decision that they thought was best for her. Joe was very upset. He couldn't go along with it. But Betty was afraid that he wouldn't stick with her through the pregnancy and she would end up in a maternity home again.

Joe felt completely helpless. He felt he should have a say in the plans for his baby. Joe couldn't sleep nights and was extremely depressed.

On the day of the abortion, Joe was sitting on a beach in California, feeling lower than he ever had in his life, he felt all alone. He felt he had no one to turn to, not even God. He turned all his anger inward and became even more depressed.

Two months later when he returned, Betty met him at the plane. "Can't we start over again?" she asked, trying to discount everything that had happened. Joe felt completely devalued. Inside, his spirit raged. Their relationship was not the same anymore. The innocence of their love had been violated.

Joe asked Betty about the procedure. She told him she aborted the baby in the toilet and then flushed it away. Joe grew sick as he pictured his baby being flushed into the city sewer system.

Why didn't Joe break up with Betty at that time? Because he still loved her. He wondered if something was wrong with him because he had been so affected by the abortion and she hadn't been. Feeling an obligation to her, even though his tenderness for her wasn't the same, he married her a year later.

Joe expressed a desire to have another child. When the child was born, they sat in the recovery room and sobbed together. After all these years of waiting, they now had the child they had long awaited. It seemed that many of the tears were for the aborted baby.

Then Betty became pregnant again. A few months into the pregnancy, the doctor told them that he thought the baby was dead. He instructed them to wait another month and allow the baby to abort naturally, but it didn't. The doctor tried to induce labor, but it didn't work. He then decided to remove the baby by Caesarean section. All of the old fears about the abortion surfaced. Joe was afraid that they were taking another child away from him, and he worried about what they were doing to his wife.

When a chaplain came to see Betty and Joe, they both sobbed. "I'm sorry," Betty told Joe. "I never meant to do this to you," (referring to his pain about the abortion).

Today Betty and Joe are in the process of getting a divorce. Betty always wanted Joe to forget about the abortion and forgive her. Joe never could forget it. And he couldn't handle Betty's seeming nonchalance. She didn't seem to think the abortion was wrong. The abortion had driven a wedge in their marriage.

Since his separation from Betty, Joe has become a Christian and has received help from the Conquerors group, where he found a nurturing and caring environment. As he shared his pain with other post-abortive men, he found some healing from his anguish.

Joe has a lot of pain and grief over the loss of two children and his wife, whom he loved very much. Only God can help reconcile the many differences they have. Joe is working on letting go of the anger and betrayal he feels. He knows he needs to forgive her and be forgiven for his attitude toward her. Joe hopes that one day they will get together again.

Dave Felt Too Weak to Stop the Abortion

Some men feel they can't say anything when their girlfriends or wives want an abortion. Even though they could have input, they don't feel emotionally strong enough to stand up for what they believe. Or they feel that if they do, their wives won't listen to them. Dave was one of these men.

Although Dave grew up in a Christian home, his parents seemed unable to give him the love and nurturing he needed. To add to this pain, he was sexually abused by a female baby-sitter. Because of these experiences, he developed a non-assertive, passive personality.

In college he met Martha, and their relationship quickly escalated into an unhealthy co-dependency. They married, but their relationship was not a strong one. Martha missed her parents, who lived several hundred miles away. She decided that if they had a baby, their marriage would improve.

Dave was afraid he couldn't be a good parent because he hadn't had good nurturing from his own parents. After the baby came, his fears were realized. Instead of making the marriage better, the child added more stress.

Two-and-a-half years later, Martha became pregnant again, but she wanted an abortion because they were struggling financially. Her parents were pushing for an abortion, as well. Dave didn't feel strong enough to speak up against both his wife and his in-laws, so he went along with the decision. Many times Dave wanted to talk with Martha about not having the abortion, but he couldn't find the courage. He was afraid it would cause more conflict in their marriage.

Martha made an appointment at a clinic in the city where her parents lived. Martha's mom went with Martha and Dave to the clinic for the procedure. Dave was frightened of the doctors and hated the fact that his child's life was going to be taken. Although he wanted to know more about the procedure, he was afraid to ask any questions.

When the abortion was over, the three of them got into the car and rode home in silence. In the many years following, Dave talked to Martha about the abortion only three times, but the pain was always there.

Although Dave and Martha gave birth to two more children, their marriage relationship continued to deteriorate until his suppressed anger exploded in violent behavior. Finally, after repeated outbursts, Martha took the children and left him.

Dave became suicidal and decided he needed counseling. Dave finally expressed his grief and guilt over the abortion that he felt he should have prevented sixteen years earlier. His counselors encouraged him to get in touch with the feelings he had. In a role-play situation, he named his aborted child Amy and envisioned her in the room with him. He told her he was sorry that he didn't stop her from being killed. This interaction began Dave's healing, which has continued as he has shared his feelings in the Conquerors men's group.

In this support group, Dave has begun to deal with the pain over the losses in his life—the loss of emotional support in his childhood, the loss of his child, and the loss of his relationship to his wife. He also is developing assertiveness, the ability to stand up for his personal convictions in such areas as abortion and relationships to women. In addition, he is working on his feelings of shame and guilt by accepting God's forgiveness and not putting himself down.

MEN WHO WERE INVOLVED IN THE ABORTION DECISION

Other post-abortive men deal with the pain and guilt of having pushed for the abortion of their child. Some felt abortion was the only way out of a desperate situation.

Others felt abortion was morally acceptable. After denying for years that they experienced any pain from the abortion, many men find their abortion experience affects their relationships to women and leaves them with feelings of guilt, shame, remorse, and anger.

Lyle Pushed for an Abortion

Lyle grew up in a small, white community, and his family showed him a lot of love and care. When Lyle was a college freshman, he brought home a girl to meet his parents. His parents gave her a cool reception. Lyle was hurt, but he got the message that having a girlfriend was not okay. His parents wanted him to excel in school, not in relationships to girls. Lyle resented their rigid, overprotective ways.

Then Lyle met Sarah, a black woman who was intelligent, sensitive, and caring. They soon started dating. Lyle felt protective of Sarah, wanting to shield her from some of the racial prejudice she was experiencing at the predominantly white college they attended. Before long the relationship became a sexual one.

Lyle knew better than to bring Sarah home to meet his parents. Not only did they disapprove of his dating, they were also racially prejudiced.

When news reached Lyle's hometown that he was dating a black girl, his father showed up on campus in a rage. "You break off this relationship, or you will be in more trouble than you've ever seen," he threatened. Lyle didn't break off the relationship, and in the fall of Lyle's senior year Sarah became pregnant.

Neither Lyle nor Sarah wanted a baby at that time. Sarah had planned to get a graduate degree, and a baby would interfere with that. They both knew that Lyle's parents would never accept Sarah and certainly not a racially mixed child.

Neither person wanted an abortion, but Lyle decided it was the only choice. Sarah went along with what he wanted. Lyle took Sarah to a nearby city to have the abortion. Both felt very uncomfortable about being in such a cold, calculating place. Lyle felt the clinic had an air of death. Sarah clung to Lyle for moral support. After she went in for the abortion, Lyle sat waiting in silence. He couldn't wait for the procedure to be over so he could leave. When the door of the recovery room opened, Sarah stood there looking pale and drained. Managing a slight smile, she said, "Take me home." As they drove back to school, neither of them talked about the abortion.

After two weeks it seemed that their relationship was back to normal. Lyle didn't realize how deeply Sarah was hurting until one night a friend told him that Sarah had taken an overdose of drugs. When he arrived at the hospital, he asked her why. She said, "You know why I did it." That was all that was said.

Two months later Lyle graduated from college and moved. Sarah was still having trouble dealing with the abortion, and Lyle was trying to give her support. About a year after the abortion, they broke off the relationship.

Two years after breaking up with Sarah, Lyle became a Christian. Realizing that he was missing something in his life, he accepted Christ to fill the void. For the first time, Lyle experienced some relief from the guilt and shame of the abortion. Then he started praying for a Christian woman who would accept him and give him support in spite of his past experiences. Within six months God brought him Jill.

After dating Jill for three months, Lyle finally got up enough nerve to tell her about the abortion. Jill understood.

She told him that she too had had an abortion. Although they both regretted the abortions in their past, they were able to comfort and support each other.

Jill and Lyle married a couple of years later. While Jill was carrying their first child, she became very depressed. All the pain, guilt, and shame of her abortion experience surfaced. Jill's parents had pushed her into having an abortion, and all her anger and resentment toward them and herself became overwhelming. She sought help through the Conquerors program.

Today both Jill and Lyle have been through the Conquerors groups and have taken leadership in this ministry. God has given them deep compassion for women and men who have been damaged by abortion.

Lyle says that the Conquerors program has helped him personally in several ways. He has learned to identify his feelings and how they change from day to day. He has become aware of how to depend on God's power in difficult circumstances. He has learned to grieve about the loss of his child. It was painful for him to acknowledge that if he had been strong enough to stand up to his parents, he would have a fourteen-year-old child today.

Lyle feels he still needs to work on the area of forgiveness. He has accepted God's forgiveness of him, realizing that God doesn't condemn him for his actions because Jesus' blood paid the penalty for all his sin. But he would like someday to contact Sarah and ask her forgiveness for putting pressure on her to have an abortion. Lyle also still struggles with his inability to forgive his parents. He feels that their judgmental, rigid, non-accepting attitudes contributed to the abortion decision.

Steve Saw Abortion As Acceptable Birth Control

Although Steve lived close to the Lord when he was a young child, he threw off his beliefs when he entered the university, adopting liberal views on abortion and other social issues. While at the university, Steve met and later married Peggy, who was studying to be a doctor.

Then one day Peggy thought she was pregnant. They decided to get an abortion. It seemed the only thing to do at the time. They had heard it was a perfectly safe alternative to pregnancy, and it seemed the logical solution. When they went to an abortion clinic, they found out she wasn't really pregnant, but they had already made up their mind that if she became pregnant, she would have an abortion.

Some time later Peggy found out she was pregnant, and they scheduled an abortion. Steve says, "I couldn't imagine another alternative. It seemed like the least painful thing to do." Steve was concerned that having to care for a baby would be too much of a burden for Peggy along with going to school and other responsibilities.

Having rationalized that abortion was okay, he actually became a defender of abortion, even getting involved politically. But when Peggy became pregnant a second time, Steve said he couldn't let her get another abortion. He talked her out of it, convincing her that since they were married, he felt God wanted them to have this child.

The pregnancy was a nightmare. Peggy experienced severe morning sickness and developed toxemia during the latter part of her pregnancy, during which time she was also studying for important exams. After three days of labor, their daughter was born, and despite all the complications, she became a real joy to them.

A year later Peggy became pregnant again, and the prospect of another baby seemed too much. Peggy felt she couldn't go through all that again. But Steve told her, "If you get an abortion, I want you to get sterilized, too. I can't go through another abortion, either." Peggy did have an abortion and also had her tubes tied. Both she and Steve felt sad about the whole situation. They both had a relationship to the Lord, but it was rather weak at this point.

Through a pro-life activist ministry, Steve and Peggy realized that abortion wasn't a gray issue. It was violence to a small person. In the past two years, their spiritual life has grown significantly, making them even more aware of their own negative feelings about abortion.

Within the last few months, Steve and his wife have communicated openly about the abortion and their feelings. They realized that these issues were never resolved. When they learned about the Conquerors groups, they decided it would be good for both of them to attend.

God impressed on Steve and Peggy that he had given them three opportunities to have children and they had killed two of these babies. So they felt they should adopt two. They know they can't buy redemption through these two children, but they know they have the financial means and the room in their hearts to care for more children. "I knew it was not within our rights to say that we shouldn't have children. Adoption was a way to fulfill God's plan for us." Steve and Peggy have already adopted one child and plan to adopt another to bring the number of their children to three again.

Through listening to stories of men in his Conquerors group, Steve saw clearly the deception they had all been a part of. The Conquerors program also helped Steve work through his shame. He says, "I now have a fuller understanding of God's forgiveness. Even though I know I will always bear the scars of the abortion, I know that God has forgiven me, and my life feels so much better."

PART IV

Nine Steps to Recovery

11

Recognizing My Powerlessness

Step 1: I recognize that I am powerless to heal the damage my abortion has caused in my life. I look to God for the power to make me whole.

The key to healing and wholeness comes in recognizing that we are powerless to heal ourselves and that only God can heal us. Yet giving up that power is difficult for us to do. We often find ourselves hindered in three ways: we think we can do it by ourselves; we don't know where to go for power for healing; and we find it difficult to trust God. Let's look more closely at these three hindrances.

OUR ATTEMPTS TO HEAL OURSELVES

Many post-abortive women and men feel that because they got themselves into the abortion experience, they are responsible to get themselves out of the pain. They look to certain behaviors to bring about healing.

147

Perfectionism

One of the most common ways that post-abortive women or men try to heal themselves is by trying to be perfect. They feel that if they do everything right, say the right things, act the right way, then they will be okay; they will have successfully handled the healing process. The problem with that philosophy is that they can't maintain the façade of perfection for very long. When they fail, they become devastated because all the pain is still there.

Christian women and men may try to heal themselves through a type of spiritual perfectionism. Trying to be "good Christians," they may become fanatical about church attendance and other Christian disciplines. While these things are essential to a vibrant Christian experience, if the women and men have not faced the pain and sin they have buried, bringing their feelings to the surface, all their religious deeds will not help the healing process.

Busyness

A second way women and men try to heal themselves is through busyness. They rationalize, "If you shove your pain down and stay busy with your job, your children, your church, and the pro-life movement, time will heal all." They believe the old adage, "Forget about it, and it will go away." But it doesn't. Painful thoughts about the abortion start popping up at unexpected times. Busyness only prolongs the pain.

If these same women and men had a physical problem such as a persistent pain in the stomach, they wouldn't say to themselves, "If only I can stay busy, then the pain will go away." Instead, they would go to a competent physician and trust in that professional's expertise and wisdom for diagnosis and treatment.

WHERE CAN WE FIND POWER FOR HEALING?

If we come to the conclusion that we are powerless to heal ourselves, are we defeated? Should we give up? Our society would like us to believe that admitting powerlessness is admitting defeat. Society values power, not powerlessness.

But God's ideas are different. He knows that when we recognize our powerlessness, we take the first step toward healing. Only if we admit that we are totally unable to bring about wholeness in our lives will we begin to look up to him for the power we need.

God doesn't see powerlessness as weakness; he sees it as his opportunity to reveal to us his strength. In the New Testament, Jesus says, "Apart from me you can do nothing" (John 15:5). God is our only source of power and healing.

When the apostle Paul realized his own weaknesses, he begged the Lord to take away those weak areas. But instead of removing Paul's weaknesses, the Lord saw them as a prerequisite for power: "My grace is sufficient for you, for *my power* is made perfect in [your] weakness." At that point, Paul accepted his powerlessness, saying, "Therefore, I will boast all the more gladly about my weaknesses, so that *Christ's power* may rest on me. . . . For when I am weak, then I am strong" (2 Cor. 12:9–10, emphasis added).

God offers post-abortive women and men unlimited power. He offers them "his incomparably great *power* . . . the working of his *mighty strength* which he accomplished in Christ when he raised him from the dead" (Eph. 1:19, emphasis added).

What Does God's Power Do?

When post-abortive women or men acknowledge their powerlessness and look to God, he supplies the power and strength needed in the emotional and spiritual healing process. God gives them power to comprehend what he can do in their lives, what incomprehensible power he can give them to find healing. God is "able to do immeasurably more than all we ask or imagine, according to his *power* that is at work within us" (Eph. 3:20, emphasis added).

God's power also gives post-abortive women and men purpose in their lives. Many women and men feel that the sin of their abortion has robbed them of a meaningful future. They may feel their lives are over. But God has a plan for their future. In Jeremiah 29:11–13, God says, "I know the plans I have for you . . . plans to prosper you and not to harm you, plans to give you hope and a future. Then you will call upon me and come and pray to me, and I will listen to you. You will seek me and find me when you seek me with all your heart."

DIFFICULTY IN TRUSTING GOD

Some post-abortive women and men feel they don't have the strength to trust God. They need to know that God understands their weaknesses. "As a father has compassion on his children, so the Lord has compassion on those who fear him; for he knows how we are formed, he remembers that we are dust" (Ps. 103:13–14).

They will be encouraged to know that as they come to him for his healing touch, he will give them the strength they need to work through the pain of their abortion experience. "Those who hope in the Lord will renew their strength. They will soar on wings like eagles; they will run and not grow weary, they will walk and not be faint" (Isa. 40:31).

Spiritual Need

Other post-abortive women or men may have trouble trusting God for healing because they have never trusted him as Savior. Jesus said, "Whoever hears my word and believes him who sent me has eternal life and will not be condemned; he has crossed over from death to life" (John 5:24). The Bible says that all of us have sinned. We can't measure up to God's holy standard. But Jesus Christ, the only perfect person who ever lived, sacrificed himself to pay the penalty for our sin. All we have to do is admit our sin to God, believe that his death was for us, and accept his free gift of eternal life. John 1:12 says that "to all who received him, to those who believed in his name [trusted in him], he gave the right to become children of God." Jesus further assures us, whoever "comes to me I will never drive away" (1 John 6:37b). We do not need to fear his judgment. Romans 8:1 says, "There is now no condemnation for those who are in Christ Jesus."

Family Relationships

Post-abortive women and men who came from families in which people didn't know how to trust one another may have trouble trusting God or anyone else. If they had no role models to show them how to trust God in daily situations, they won't know how to develop a trusting relationship to him, no matter how much they may desire it.

Control

Trusting God is extremely difficult for women or men who have a strong need to be in control. They are afraid that if they surrender the control of their lives to God, they may lose something important to them. They worry about what they will have to give up.

Being powerless before God doesn't mean that you should allow others to take advantage of you. It does mean that through God you have the power to overcome life's pain, and it is he who gives you the strength to be assertive.

Distorted Image of God

Many post-abortive women and men have a distorted image of God, as we have mentioned in chapter 8. They believe that God wants only to punish them for their sins. In the Conquerors support group, however, women and men are encouraged to pray for God's help in letting go of their fears and wrong perceptions of him. As others in the group share how they are working through this issue, women and men observe the healing the others are experiencing and gain more confidence that God can do it in their lives too. They learn a great deal about God's true nature as others in the group support them in love and unconditional acceptance. Studying Scripture further empowers them to learn God's truth and apply it to their lives.

As the post-abortive women and men experience God's healing, they will become more aware of his presence in their lives and also come to understand his love. Paul told the Ephesians that all of Christ's power was at their disposal. He prayed this prayer for them: "May [he] strengthen you with *power* through his Spirit in your inner being, so that Christ may dwell in your hearts through faith. And I pray that you, being rooted and established in love, may have *power,* together with all the saints to grasp how wide and long and high and deep is the love of Christ, and to know that this love surpasses knowledge—that you may be filled to the measure of all the fullness of God" (Eph. 3:16–19, emphasis added).

When post-abortive women and men tap the rich resources of Christ's power, they will find their faith stimulated and their experience of God's love more real.

We encourage Conquerors women and men to express their personal feelings creatively as they work through the healing process. Some express themselves through artwork while others write poetry, journal entries, life stories, and letters to God or those who have hurt them.

After God touched Becky, a Conquerors group member, with his love and compassion, she began experiencing release from the spiritual and emotional pain following her abortion. The Lord helped her find freedom and a renewed life. She wrote the following poem as an expression of the beauty God brought out of her pain.

GOD TOOK MY TEARS

God took my tears
and made cascading waterfalls.
Out of the land flattened and hollowed out by my pain,
God grew a meadow overflowing with flowers.
God tore down the mountains of my independence
so that I would come to Him to reach all heights.
After the forest fire of my own anger and unforgiving spirit,
young saplings emerged one day.
Then God opened the cave where I had hid all of the ugliness,
and roses grew with the light.
Out of the storms created by my confusion and uncertainty
came a sea of love and a river of compassion.

HOMEWORK QUESTIONS

All of the remaining chapters ask you to do some reflective writing—in the form of both homework questions and other reflective activities. You may want to keep all of your work in one notebook, perhaps a ringbinder, so that you can keep your responses in one place and add to your notebook any articles or other resources you may want to keep.

1. In what areas of your life do you need healing?

2. In the past how have you tried to heal yourself from your abortion experience? How well has this worked?

3. What does it mean to be powerless?

4. How do you feel when you think about acknowledging your own powerlessness?

5. How do you see God? Where did these ideas come from?

6. How do you think God sees you?

7. What has happened in your past that might hinder you from trusting God for your healing process?

8. Take the first step toward your healing. Admit to God and to yourself that you are powerless. Then ask him to give you his healing power. Practice this surrender and this request every day.

12

Identifying My Feelings

Step 2: I will identify my feelings related to my abortion experience. I will start by exploring my feelings of fear and anxiety and my feelings of anger toward myself and others. I will acknowledge how these feelings have affected my life, and with God's help I will seek inner peace.*

In order for healing to begin, post-abortive women and men need to recognize their feelings and fuse God's truth with the things they are experiencing. But sometimes they can't identify what their feelings are. They have a vague idea, but they can't really name the feelings.

IDENTIFYING MY FEELINGS

Use the following feelings-awareness assessment to help you pinpoint what feelings you've had as the result of your

---

*This step is usually taught in two different meetings: one meeting devoted to Part One: Fear and Anxiety, the other to Part Two: Anger.

abortion experience and all the circumstances surrounding that experience. In your homework notebook, make a three-columned list of feelings you've had: include in column 1 primary feelings, ones that have persisted over a long period of time; include in column 2 secondary feelings, ones that you have felt often but not as intensely as those in column 1; include in column 3 feelings you've had occasionally.

FEELINGS-AWARENESS ASSESSMENT

abandoned	constructive	exhilarated
accepted	contented	exploited
adequate	controlled	fascinated
adventurous	cowardly	fearful
affected	damned	flighty
afraid	defeated	foolish
alone	defensive	forlorn
ambivalent	defiant	free
angry	dependent	frustrated
anxious	desirous	full
apathetic	despairing	glad
apprehensive	despondent	graceful
ashamed	disappointed	graceless
awed	discontented	grateful
awkward	discouraged	great
bewildered	distracted	guilty
bold	disturbed	gullible
bored	down	gutsy
calm	dull	happy
captivated	eager	hateful
caring	elated	helpless
cautious	embarrassed	hesitant
cheated	empathetic	high
clownish	empty	hopeful
cold	enchanted	hopeless
comfortable	encouraged	hostile
compelled	energized	humble
concerned	envious	hurt
confident	exasperated	impatient
congenial	excited	important

indifferent
inferior
intolerant
irrational
irritated
isolated
jealous
joyful
kind
knocked down
let down
lonely
loved
lovely
miserable
naked
natural
nervous
numb
obligated
overcome
overwhelmed
pained
peaceful
pious
pitied
pleased
poised

possessive
proud
provoked
pushed
put out
rational
refreshed
regretful
rejected
relieved
reluctant
remorseful
resentful
resigned
respectable
revengeful
satisfied
secure
selfish
self-pitying
shy
sick
snappy
stubborn
stunned
stupid
successful
sucked in

suffering
superior
surprised
surrendered
suspicious
sympathetic
tired
tranquil
trapped
uncomfortable
understood
uneasy
unhappy
unloved
unmasked
unsure
unworthy
used
victimized
violated
warm
weary
withdrawn
witty
wonderful
worried
worthy

If you are like most post-abortive women and men, you will find that feelings you listed in column 1 are forms of fear, anxiety, or anger. Let's examine your fear and anxiety.

PART ONE: FEAR AND ANXIETY

What are fear and anxiety? How do they manifest themselves in our lives? And how can we find release from their power?

Fear

Fear is a feeling of danger or fright that is attributed to some specific experience, person, or thing. In chapter 7, for instance, we noted that post-abortive women often are afraid of medical exams, sexual intercourse, medical personnel, sounds of abortion, disclosure, God's punishment, and future infertility. In the Conquerors women's survey, women noted a variety of things they feared: 22.1 percent said they feared people (80.1 percent said this fear began after the abortion experience); 16.2 percent expressed a fear of crowds (81.9 percent said this fear started after the abortion).

Extreme fear—phobias. When people's fears become extreme, they develop phobias. They become inordinately fearful of some object or situation (which usually does not present any threat to them), avoiding it at all cost.

Phobias restrict peoples choices, forcing them into rigid behaviors that isolate them from social contact with others. For instance, post-abortive women and men may have difficulty leaving their home (as in agoraphobia—the fear of open places).

Anxiety

Anxiety is a concern or worry that does not have a particular target. It is more vague and indiscernible. Anxiety also lasts longer than fear. It hangs on. *The New Webster's Universal Encyclopedia* defines anxiety as: "Generalized pervasive fear. Anxiety is partly the feeling of apprehension, partly the behavior of avoiding frightening situations, and partly the associated bodily changes, such as sweating, a fast pulse, and tense muscles."[1]

Cheri, a Conquerors group leader, has suffered from

post-abortion trauma, and her story exemplifies many of the symptoms post-abortive women and men experience. She describes her understanding of the difference between fear and anxiety.

> It's like you are going to the dentist for a root canal. You've had root canals before so you expect pain and discomfort. On the way to the office, you pass someone you know. You make eye contact, but that person doesn't acknowledge you in any way—just passes by. Anxiety sets in, but it is pushed to the background while you are at the dentist. Although fear is much stronger than anxiety, fear disappears as soon as the dentist is done. The anxiety remains—lurking, gnawing at you during your wakeful hours and slipping in and out of your troubled dreams at night. You worry why the person didn't speak to you.

Conquerors women and men recognize that they feel fear and anxiety related to their abortion experience. Most women and men experience mild, normal fear and anxiety brought on by the stress they have been under and the secret they live with. Women and men suffering from generalized anxiety are unable to pinpoint exactly what they are afraid of. A significant number of Conquerors women (23.5 percent) stated that they suffered from non-specific fears, and 74.3 percent of these women said that these fears came *after* their abortion experience.

Generalized anxiety perpetuates a persistent sense of tension and dread. The person may be constantly on edge, waiting for something terrible to happen. For example, some of the Conquerors women live in fear that something is going to happen to their children or that they will never be able to have a child. These women may find it hard to concentrate, make decisions, or remember appointments.

Other women and men struggle with more severe anxiety, which can become incapacitating. These women and men will need more intensive counseling than what the Conquerors group can provide.

In their book *Worry-Free Living,* Minirth, Meier, and Hawkins talk about the difference between normal and abnormal anxiety:

> It's a fine line that separates normal anxiety from the abnormal variety. *Much depends on how intense the anxiety is, how long it lasts, what brings it on in the first place, and how frequently it returns.* Positive anxiety is an asset, a built-in alarm system that signals possible danger. . . . Negative anxiety, on the other hand, is an alarm system with its wires crossed—it goes off for the wrong reason (or for no reason at all), at the wrong times, and often can't be silenced. This kind of anxiety isn't a *warning* of danger, but a danger itself.[2]

Serious anxiety can take the form of panic attacks, obsessive thoughts, compulsive behavior, and depression.

Panic attacks. Intense anxiety may lead to panic attacks. When anxiety rises to an unbearable level, you may begin to feel dizzy and shaky. You may feel your pulse quicken, your heart pound, and your lungs gasp for breath. Although these attacks usually last for only a few minutes, you may feel exhausted afterward. Cheri describes her panic attacks: "I found myself having trouble driving, especially using freeway ramps. I would actually imagine the impact of a car hitting me as I pulled onto the freeway, even though I allowed much more space than I needed. When I was driving, I could see the cars all coming straight toward me. At times I developed a full panic attack—very high anxiety level, hyperventilating, sweaty palms, impaired vision, and pain in my head. I was almost paralyzed with fear."

Obsessive thoughts. Anxiety may manifest itself through obsessive thoughts. Obsessive thoughts are more than persistent thoughts that leave within a few minutes or hours. Obsessive thoughts recur for days, months, and years at a time. Excessive guilt feelings may underlay obsessive thoughts. Cheri knows what it's like to struggle with obsessions. She says, "Obsessions led me to become rigid, inflexible, perfectionistic, overly conscientious, and possessive of things and people. I saw everything as black or white, good or bad. I got very tired, weary from the enormous amount of energy obsessing takes."

Obsessive thoughts torment the person night and day, often causing sleep difficulties. Cheri relates this to her abortion experience: "I remember lying in bed at night, thinking about the abortion over and over—about the clinic, the doctor, how I was treated. I would question my decision, debating it over and over in my head."

Compulsive behavior. Anxiety also may manifest itself in compulsive behavior—ritualistic, repetitive behavior like constant hand washing or constant checking to make sure a door is locked. A compulsive person feels an all-consuming drive to do these things and is very anxious if she or he is prevented from engaging in the ritual. People with compulsive behavior patterns need professional help from counselors or groups that deal specifically with this behavior disorder.

Depression. Anxiety also manifests itself in depression. Minirth, Meier, and Hawkins discuss the relationship between anxiety and depression. "Just as people confuse anxiety and fear, so do they have trouble distinguishing between anxiety and depression. Here's the difference: Anxiety is more linked to the future, and depression is connected more directly with the past. Or, put another way, *anxiety is the future superimposed on the present, and depression is the past superimposed on the present.*"[3]

Post-abortive women and men often repress the anxiety, fear, pain, guilt, and shame they feel about their abortion experience. Repressing these feelings does not help them go away. In fact, repression often causes those past feelings to encroach on present experiences—"the past superimposed on the present"—or depression. If these feelings are not resolved, the depression often will be a long-term one.

RELEASE FROM FEAR AND ANXIETY

The good news is that post-abortive women and men can find release from fear and anxiety. We've already discussed the first step: identifying the feelings and acknowledging that they have power over you. Face those feelings head on and realistically assess what impact they've had on your life.

Cheri uses an analogy to explain the importance of dealing with these feelings: "Rather than ignoring our pain, it is healthier to endure the pain of the truth long enough to heal the wound causing it. We make the choice. It is like merely covering a cut with a Band-Aid. If we leave the Band-Aid on, doing nothing about the cut, it begins to hurt, redden, fester, and swell. Pus begins to ooze out around the Band-Aid. When we finally take the Band-Aid off, we need to cleanse the wound thoroughly before it can heal."

The second step is to share those fears and anxieties with a counselor, with your support group, and especially with God. "Cast all your anxiety on him because he cares for you" (1 Peter 5:7).

Third, post-abortive women and men need to identify the defense mechanisms (the Band-Aids in Cheri's analogy) that they have used to cover up the pain of the abortion (chapter 15 will discuss defense mechanisms more thoroughly). In the following list, identify any defense mechanisms you may have used to deny your feelings.

DEFENSE MECHANISMS

agreeableness	flightiness	projection
ambivalence	flippancy	rationalization
antagonism	generalizing	repression
compliance	intellectualization	self-contempt
conformity	perfectionism	silence
defensiveness	procrastination	talkativeness
denial		

Fourth, anxious women and men need to look to God's Word for help in decreasing their anxiety. It is not God's plan for them to be filled with fear and anxiety. "For God did not give us a spirit of [fear], but a spirit of power, of love and of self-discipline" (2 Tim. 1:7).

Principles for Decreasing Anxiety

In their book, *Happiness Is a Choice,* Frank Minirth and Paul Meier give ten principles for decreasing anxiety. Basing their principles on Philippians 4, they make these suggestions.

1. Determine to obey God's command. Philippians says that we are not to "be anxious about anything" (v. 6).

2. Pray. "In everything, by prayer and petition, with thanksgiving, present your requests to God" (v. 6).

3. Realize that God can keep our minds safe as we obey him. "The peace of God, which transcends all understanding, will guard your hearts and your minds in Christ Jesus" (v. 7).

4. Meditate on positive thoughts. "Whatever is true, whatever is noble, whatever is right, whatever is pure, whatever is lovely, whatever is admirable—if anything is excellent or praiseworthy—think about such things" (v. 8). Stop, relax. Anxiety is a signal to relax. Meditate on a verse like Philippians 4:8. Listen to soothing music. Take a walk in a beautiful park. Read an uplifting book. Spend some time with a godly, encouraging friend. Sing about God's goodness and faithfulness.

5. Focus on godly behavior. "Whatever you have learned or received or heard from me, or seen in me—put it into practice. And the God of peace will be with you" (v. 9).

6. Divert attention from self to others. Paul commended the Philippians for getting their minds off themselves and thinking about others (v. 10).

7. Work on being content. Paul says, "I have learned to be content whatever the circumstances" (v. 11). Even though your circumstances may seem to be dreadful and hopeless, learn to find contentment in what you *do* have this day, this hour. Learn to see God's goodness in the worst of situations.

8. Realize there is a twofold responsibility (yours and Christ's) in doing anything. "I can do everything through [Christ] who gives me strength" (v. 13). An individual can overcome anxiety through Christ.

9. Eliminate the fear of poverty. "My God will meet all your needs according to his glorious riches in Christ Jesus" (v. 19).

10. Realize that the grace of God is with you. "The grace of the Lord Jesus Christ be with your spirit" (v. 23).[4]

In addition, Minirth and Meier suggest the following practical ingredients for overcoming anxiety: Listen to Christian music; get adequate sleep, exercise, and recreation; live a day at a time; develop open relationships where you can share your feelings; avoid procrastination; imagine a worst-case scenario and think through how you would deal with it; and set a limit on your worries.[5]

This last suggestion may seem unusual, but it has been very effective in my counseling experience. Minirth and Meier say, "We encourage [people] to set aside a definite period of time each day, such as fifteen minutes in the evening, to consider and order whatever their particular problem might be."[6] If they start to worry at other times during the day, they should tell themselves that they can worry later that night. That's their prescribed time to worry.

HOMEWORK QUESTIONS

1. If you have not yet made your list from the Feelings-Awareness Assessment, do that now. How was the assessment helpful to you?

2. Are you aware of ways in which you have suppressed feelings related to your abortion? If so, in what ways have you done this?

3. Which of the Conquerors nine steps do you most fear working through?

4. How has your life been affected by fear and anxiety (i.e., lack of confidence, missed opportunities, unhealthy relationships, physical symptoms, etc.)?

5. Ask yourself: Is anxiety an unwelcome companion in my life? If so, where does the root of my anxiety lie?

6. What do you believe you need to do to be released from the grip of anxiety or fear? What do you need to entrust to God?

7. For five days this week, take two of the ten principles suggested by Minirth and Meier and practice them during the day.

8. Using a Bible concordance, find several Scripture passages that you can use for serious meditation about releasing your fears and anxieties to God. Share some of these passages with other people in your support group.

PART TWO: ANGER

Anger in itself is not wrong. The Bible, for instance, does not prohibit anger. But it does recognize that anger can easily lead to sin. We can choose to use our feelings of anger constructively or destructively.

Constructive Anger

Jesus expressed constructive (righteous) anger at the moneychangers who had turned the temple in Jerusalem into a noisy marketplace (see John 2:14–16). Jesus could see that the merchants' hearts and activities were not pleasing to God, and he used his anger in a constructive way to bring about change.

Post-abortive women and men who have come to see that abortion is wrong may have righteous anger about the mass slaughter of the unborn. This anger could lead them to speak out constructively against abortion or to work in a crisis pregnancy center, helping young women choose life for the unborn.

Destructive Anger

But too often our anger is destructive, leading to bitterness and hatred. Paul warns, "In your anger do not sin. Do not let the sun go down while you are still angry, and do not give the devil a foothold" (Eph. 4:26–27). This leads us to believe that when we get angry and harbor that anger, the devil gets a foothold in our life. Hebrews 12:15 tells us to be watchful, "that no bitter root grows up to cause trouble and defile many." Holding on to anger leads to resentment and causes our relationships to become "defiled."

As we noted in chapter 7, many post-abortive women indicated that they were angry not only with themselves but also with their sexual partners, with abortion providers, with other pregnant women, with children—and even with God. They respond angrily to the injustices they perceive have been done to them. If this anger is expressed in an honest way without trying to hurt someone else, it can be constructive. But if the anger is meant to harm, it is destructive. The story in chapter 10 showed how Dave's anger toward Martha for having the abortion led to deep bitterness against her.

Destructive anger can express itself in repression, depression, defensiveness, blaming, rage, and manipulation.

Repression. Some post-abortive women and men can express their anger openly. But others hold it inside, feeling it's wrong to express any anger. Many times these women and men repress their anger to the point that they are not even in touch with it.

Depression. Anger and resentment turned inward are very destructive and can result in depression (see chapter 7) and physical ailments such as ulcers, headaches, and hypertension. That's why it is important for post-abortive women and men to get in touch with these feelings and express them.

Defensiveness. Anger often expresses itself as defensiveness. If post-abortive women and men have endured traumatic abuse, they may deny ever having been angry about it.

Blaming. When post-abortive women or men become angry, they often blame someone else for their anger. They may blame their parents, spouse, boyfriend/girlfriend, or children for their predicament.

Rage. Anger also becomes destructive when it erupts in rage—when people lose control of themselves, blow up, or become physically violent. Some women and men who struggle with destructive anger allow resentment and tension to build to the point that they become violent with their children. Or they may be caught in the cycle of violence themselves, trapped by a violent relationship to a spouse. Two stories in chapter 10 tell of the destructive power of unchecked anger. Dave's anger became so destructive that he had violent outbursts that led to the breakup of his marriage. When Don learned that Pat had had an abortion without his permission, he boiled with anger and rage. His anger turned into bitterness and hatred toward both Pat and himself. People whose anger has erupted in rage and violence often need professional help.

Manipulation. Post-abortive women and men may hold on to their anger in an attempt to manipulate the people around them. They may try to make the person who pushed for the abortion pay for their pain. Or their anger can become manipulative if they use it to keep people at a distance, protecting themselves from further hurt. Some angry post-abortive women and men will manipulate others by trying to make them feel guilty for not meeting their needs. They will punish them by not talking to them, or they will try to intimidate them with explosive outbursts of yelling, screaming, or sarcasm.

Anger As a Cover

Many times anger is a cover or defense mechanism for other, unidentified feelings. Anger is often a warning signal that should alert post-abortive women and men to other emotions that may be churning underneath the anger. Anger may be a cover for hurt, betrayal, or sadness.

When post-abortive women and men recognize their anger, they should ask themselves, What are the underlying feelings or expectations that precipitated this anger? By identifying the root cause of the anger, they can better understand themselves and clearly communicate their feelings to others. Other people are more likely to listen to someone who says, "I feel hurt by you" than to someone who says, "I'm angry with you."

Anger Distorts

Anger distorts reality. Anger clouds the lens through which post-abortive women and men perceive their relationships and circumstances. These distorted perceptions may lead them to imagine hurtful motives behind what people do. Anger may lead them to see the people around them as uncaring or judgmental. Anger often intensifies conflicts they feel with other people.

Anger and Perfectionism

Many post-abortive women and men who struggle with anger expect perfection—from themselves and others. They are hard on themselves, never accepting their own limitations. They always expect more from themselves, and they are always disappointed—and angry.

Their anger and perfectionism are equally destructive when they are turned on other people. Perfectionistic women and men often expect their spouse or sexual partner to know what they want and how they feel. They assume they are entitled to immediate gratification. They also assume that if they do something nice for someone else, that person will do something nice for them. When that person doesn't reciprocate, they feel justified in their anger.

When the other people involved in these relationships give in to these unrealistic demands, they feel trapped, controlled, and exhausted. This creates a further problem for the angry people because they have alienated others and still may not get what they want.

SUGGESTIONS FOR WORKING THROUGH ANGER

1. Identify your anger. In your homework notebook, make a list of people and events that make you angry. Then rewrite the list, ranking the items in the order of intensity—from those that make you the most angry to those that make you the least angry.

2. Evaluate your anger. In order to determine whether your anger is constructive (righteous) or destructive (unrighteous), make a column of the advantages and disadvantages of feeling angry and acting in a retaliatory manner. What are the greater costs and benefits of each? You may discover that your anger seriously affects your health and impedes your effectiveness at work. You may discover that eliminating anger could result in people liking you more, a better testimony for Christ, having better self-control, and feeling better about yourself.

3. Be on guard. As you recognize thoughts that make you angry, remind yourself to shut off your mind's tape recorder. Think about something else, find someone to talk to, read the Bible or another good book, go for a walk, or jog. If you keep turning off the anger tapes in your mind, you won't be bombarded by as many reruns.

4. Let go. Learn to relax and use your humor. Be willing to let go of your perfectionistic expectations of others and yourself. Learn to accept and love people unconditionally. Rewrite the unrealistic rules that you have set for yourself and others.

5. Walk in other people's shoes. Develop empathy or an understanding of other people's reactions and behaviors. When you understand why the other person is acting that way, you will be less likely to become angry. Don't always take it personally if someone isn't talking to you. He or she may simply be having a bad day.

6. Focus on God's Word. Use Scripture verses to renew your mind and focus on God's plan for how you should treat other people. While you may find the following verses difficult to apply to your life as you are recovering from pain, nonetheless, it is important for you to work toward this goal with God's help.

> Live in harmony with one another. Do not be proud, but be willing to associate with people of low position. Do not be conceited. Do not repay anyone evil for evil. Be careful to do what is right in the eyes of everybody. If it is possible, as far as it depends upon you, live at peace with everyone. Do not take revenge, my friends, but leave room for God's wrath, for it is written: "It is mine to avenge; I will repay," says the Lord (Rom. 12:16–19).

> Finally, all of you, live in harmony with one another; be sympathetic, love as brothers, be compassionate and humble. Do not repay evil with evil or insult with insult, but with blessing, because to this you were called so that you may inherit a blessing (1 Pet. 3:8–9).

HOMEWORK QUESTIONS

1. Against whom do you harbor angry feelings for their part in your abortion?

2. What feelings accompany the anger in each of these cases? Use the Feelings-Awareness Assessment list to help you identify underlying feelings of hurt, betrayal, abandonment, rejection, or pressure.

3. What situations *contributing to* your abortion experience still make you angry?

4. What situations *stemming from* your abortion experience still make you angry?

5. In each of these instances, how has the anger affected your life?

6. Can you release your anger, or do you feel you must hold on to it? Explain.

7. Do you become physically or verbally abusive with your anger? What are you going to do about it?

13

Dealing with My Guilt and Shame

Step 3: I understand that the guilt, shame, and emotional distress I suffer may be consequences of my abortion. I will acknowledge these feelings and seek to resolve them.

WHAT IS THE DIFFERENCE BETWEEN GUILT AND SHAME?

Guilt is a healthy God-given feeling resulting from a broken biblical directive. It is related to a specific event and does not damage the person's self-esteem. Guilt is a signal that we have missed the mark—God's mark. It reminds us that we are imperfect yet worthwhile people who are able to learn from our mistakes and grow as individuals. Guilt is cured through repentance and forgiveness.

Shame is an emotional problem rooted in our childhood. Many women and men who struggle with shame were raised in homes where their emotional and nurturing needs were not met, and they were not valued as individuals.

GUILT

King David is a perfect example of a person struggling with guilt over sin. In Psalm 32 he talks about the guilt he experienced when he committed adultery and murder. When David confessed his sin, God forgave him and David was able to resolve his guilt.

Women and men who feel guilt because of an abortion often find it difficult to accept forgiveness. They feel as if they have committed an unpardonable sin. Even though they know that God can forgive them, they may not be able to forgive themselves. They may persistently pursue the career goals that led them to the abortion, even though these goals aren't as important to them anymore. It is as if they have to prove that their reasons for aborting the baby were valid ones. They may become involved in helping others through the pro-life movement or the pro-choice movement as Dawn did (chapter 1). Or they may volunteer to help in service organizations, often with children.

They always will try to live up to their perfectionistic standards. And they always will fail. They will never be perfect or do enough good things to find acceptance from God and others. Then they will blame themselves for failing. The vicious cycle of guilt will be broken only when they are able to confess their sin, find their self-worth in Jesus Christ, and accept his love and forgiveness.

Lori's story illustrates how the Lord can release a post-abortive woman or man from guilt:

Lori's Story

"I coped with my abortion by stuffing my feelings so deeply inside of myself that I honestly did not know they were there anymore. But those emotions had become a festering sore inside of me, ready to ooze out at the most inappropriate times. I found myself feeling guilt every time I heard the word *abortion*. Any news coverage of pro-life activities left a churning in my stomach. I felt inferior to women in my church group. I was sure no other woman there could have done what I did. I began isolating myself—always feeling that somehow they could tell I was a worthless being.

"One day the Lord led me to talk about my abortion with a close friend who was a volunteer at New Life Family Services. I was afraid my confession would end our friendship, but the urge to talk to her was so strong, I couldn't avoid it. Much to my surprise, she revealed that she also had had an abortion. We cried and talked. It was such a relief finally to talk with someone who understood what I was going through.

"My friend invited me to a Conquerors group. I felt I had worked through my abortion and didn't need this, but I didn't want to disappoint my friend, so I went. It didn't take long to realize how desperately I needed help. As I went through the nine steps, the seeds of healing were sown. I began to realize how *only God* could heal me. I could see how my guilt was slowly destroying my life. Most of all, I realized that God really had forgiven me and I could begin to forgive myself. I felt as if a floodgate of emotions had been opened up. With the loving support of others in my group, I was able to begin grieving the loss of my child and find comfort as I envisioned him in the loving arms of Jesus.

"For me, the healing process is far from over. But I thank God for his love for me and for bringing me to Conquerors."

Some women and men have a hard time feeling forgiven because they confuse their feelings of emotional distress—

remorse and regret—with unforgiven guilt. They are unable to separate "I've done a bad thing" from "I feel bad." They may ask themselves, "If God has forgiven me for this, why do I feel so bad?" They need to remember that even though they've been forgiven, they will still feel the emotional consequences of what they have done. The emotional distress is natural and is similar to the scar left by a physical wound; eventually it will heal.

SHAME

Post-abortive women and men who struggle with shame can trace its roots to childhood experiences that left them feeling inadequate and worthless. They may have been emotionally or physically abused as children. But more often they were measured against other family members, criticized for not achieving what their parents desired, or put down for their behavior or appearance. They entered adulthood feeling inadequate.

Their abortion experience adds to the shaming feelings of inadequacy and worthlessness, so they try to hide their painful secret and continue to shame themselves for taking the life of their child.

Cheri is a good example of how post-abortive women and men try to overcome their shame and guilt feelings through perfectionism and achievement.

Cheri's Story

"My story actually started with a lonely little seven-year-old girl who couldn't face third grade because she couldn't write in cursive. I felt that I wasn't okay. I felt I was worthless if I wasn't a high achiever.

"This certainly was not a spoken message. It was taught

by attitude and lifestyle. My heart knew that love, acceptance, belonging, identity, and value were dependent on my
ability to perform and achieve.

"My solution? Just try harder. Eventually my goal
became perfection. By my senior year in high school, I looked
as if I had achieved it. I seemed perfect on the outside, but I
felt fearful on the inside.

"In my junior year of college, the pressure became too
much. I sought help from my counselor, pastor, and parents.
They gave me pep talks. 'Just keep trying. You'll make it,'
they said.

"I couldn't try harder anymore. I dropped out of
college. My fears were realized. My performance was gone.
My only options were perfection or nothing. I was now
nothing.

"As a nothing, I felt I no longer had a claim to anything
of *value*. For example, chastity had been a high value for me,
but I now felt I had no 'right' to even that. My lifestyle
reflected this feeling.

"When I became pregnant, I denied it. But finally I had
to face reality. The comments I had heard whenever a
classmate became pregnant rang in my ears. 'How shameful!'
'How could she do that to her parents?' 'What a disgrace to
the family!'

"Telling my family was equivalent to a ten on the
Richter scale of pain. My parents wanted to be supportive, so
I agreed to their idea of staying with my older brother's
family out of state. When I arrived at my brother's house, he
quickly had me put my car in the garage and asked me not to
answer the phone or the doorbell. He no longer invited his
friends to his house. He made me stay in the house; I couldn't
even go to church. He told me it would be easier for *me* if no

one knew I was home. I didn't feel that they supported me at all. I felt only shame.

"After the delivery, I placed my child for adoption. We never talked about it again. Life went on. Empty. Searching.

"Ten years after that crisis pregnancy, I faced another. I quickly resolved that I wouldn't face that shame again. No matter what! I told no one. I scheduled the abortion. I closed my mind.

"Abortion is a death experience. For me there were two deaths that morning—that of my child and the part of me that might have been salvageable.

"The abortion experience absolutely cemented my belief that God would never care for me. I was simply too bad. I had committed the unforgivable sin. Yet I still cried out to him. But I closed my heart to his 'I love you.'

"Five years later, the Lord sent an 'angel' who guided me to believe that God's grace was for me too. This was the beginning of life for me, of hope, of value. My new life began with just a flicker. Shame was powerfully imbedded in me, and like a bad weed, it took time to eradicate.

"I still struggle with perfectionistic, performance-based behavior. My head had an easier time understanding grace than my heart had accepting it. But recently the concept has finally begun to sink in. I can now confidently say from experience that God is an all-forgiving God. He loves the unlovable and forgives the unforgivable. He takes the broken and makes them whole. My life proves it."

Cheri understands what it means to be released from shame and guilt. Having gone through the Conquerors program, she is presently a Conquerors group leader, helping post-abortive women work through the shame and guilt of their own abortion experiences.

As Cheri's life demonstrates, women and men who have had abortions often suffer from much shame and guilt—before the abortion and afterward. Steve suffered deep shame because he and his wife, Peggy, made the decision to abort two of their children (chapter 10). He is ashamed that he believed abortion was a good option.

Defenses Against Shame

Post-abortive women and men who struggle with shame often use defenses against their feelings. The defenses may express themselves in various behaviors, from perfectionism and control to excessive busyness and addiction.

Perfectionism like Cheri's is often used as a defense against shame. Psychologist Tim Sheehan says that perfectionism is "a rigid belief system, 'a judge within,' that monitors, evaluates, and critiques our behavior, thoughts, and feelings. The judge within demands perfection. Mistakes are disastrous! We think we must achieve in all aspects of our life in order to be worthwhile. We convince ourselves that only a perfect performance will compensate for our inward feelings of shame."[1]

The flip side of perfectionism is judgmentalism. By criticizing and making other people look bad, inadequate people feel better about themselves. This defense is actually a form of spiritual abuse because the person who is judging is playing God. Only God is perfect, and only he has the right to judge others.

A third defense against shame is trying to gain power and control. In his book, *Healing the Shame That Binds You*, theologian and counselor John Bradshaw says that control is a way to ensure that no one will shame us again. He says that it involves: "controlling our own thoughts, expressions, feelings and actions. And it involves attempting to control other people's thoughts, feelings and actions. Control is the ultimate villain in destroying intimacy."[2] In trying to compensate for their shame and feelings of inadequacy, people try to exert power over others.

Still other people deal with their shame by becoming caretakers of others. While such behavior may appear to be noble and healthy, the caretaking often is the inadequate person's attempt to feel better about herself or himself.

Shame may also manifest itself in a façade of pleasant behavior that keeps others from knowing the real person. Putting on a mask of pleasantness only manipulates other people and circumstances.

Feelings of shame may provoke addictive behaviors, such as overeating or undereating, excessive alcohol or drug consumption, and sexual addictions (chapter 7). Other self-defeating behaviors may include social withdrawal and isolation, suicidal thoughts, or even suicide attempts. Dave became suicidal because of the pain, grief, and anger he had about his abortion experience. He finally had to get into treatment to receive help (chapter 10).

Jeff Van Vonderen says that if we have relationships that cause us to feel shamed or blamed, we may be interpreting life through a shame-grid: "A shame-grid causes you to receive words, external circumstances and events, and the way others treat you as an indictment—a judgment that you aren't good enough as a person. You interpret words and actions to mean more than what they really mean; in other words, you readily assume that people see you as a lesser person."[3]

Post-abortive women and men need to discover the sources of their shame and then identify the defenses they use to reduce these feelings. They need to remember that shame-based behavior can be changed.

WORK THROUGH GUILT AND SHAME

1. Deal with your guilt feelings. Working through this step can be very painful. You may feel devastated as you allow yourself to feel the guilt. You may feel overwhelmed by the reality of your abortion, the finality of it, and your accountability for it. It's important to identify the difference between feelings of guilt and feelings of shame. Remember that the cure for guilt is repentance and forgiveness. Search the Scripture for assurances of God's forgiveness. Write out one key verse that speaks clearly to you about how God has forgiven you. As you write it, change the pronouns to personal ones so that it is as if you and God are in a conversation. For example: "You, Lord, are compassionate and gracious, slow to anger and abounding in love. . . . You do not treat me as my sins deserve or repay me according to my iniquities. . . . As far as the east is from the west, so far have you removed my trangressions from me" (Ps. 103:8–12). Then memorize the verse and speak it to yourself when you are tempted to continue to feel guilty.

2. Identify shame messages. Reflect on your life, from your childhood to the present, and write down the shame messages you have been given. Write a list of the shame messages you still give yourself. You can change those messages by talking back to yourself. When you hear yourself say, "You're worthless. How could anyone respect you after what you've done?" you can reply with the positive truth about yourself: "The Bible tells me that I am precious in God's sight. I am valuable. He thinks enough of me to pay for my sin through the death of his own son. I am worthwhile because of how God sees me." Next to each shame message on your list, write a true message. Take some time to use a concordance to find

Bible verses that speak of how God sees you. Practice this "self-talk" daily. Counter the shame messages with the truth of God's Word.

3. Identify your responses to guilt and shame. What behaviors do you use to reduce these feelings? Do you resort to perfectionism, judgmentalism, control, constant busyness, or excessive sleep, sexual activity, eating, use of drugs or alcohol? Identifying your responses can help you set up a plan of action to change the non-productive behaviors.

HOMEWORK QUESTIONS

1. What is the difference between guilt and shame?

2. Shame can be used to manipulate and control others. Was your family one which used shame to control your behavior as a child? If so, how was it used?

3. What are your current sources of shame? What shaming messages are you giving yourself?

4. How do you deal with guilt and shame? What behaviors do you use to cover or reduce feelings of guilt and shame?

5. Ask yourself: What do I stand to lose or to gain by surrendering my feelings of guilt and shame to God?

14

Working Through My Grieving Process

Step 4: I will accept mourning as part of the healing process as I grieve the loss of my child. I will work through the stages of grief with the help of God.

THE GRIEVING PROCESS

Many post-abortive women and men start to grieve before they are even aware of their grief. They feel empty, purposeless, helpless. They don't recognize these feelings as symptoms of grief.

Our society doesn't help the grieving process. Because society tells us that abortion involves "ridding the body of unwanted tissues," post-abortive people are often confused by their feelings after the abortion. Why are they sad? Why do they cry a lot? Why do they feel unstable? They are told to forget the abortion and get on with their lives.

But grieving is an essential part of the healing process. Until post-abortive women and men can face their loss and grieve because of it, they will not move toward wholeness.

Post-abortive women and men need help with the grieving process. First, they need to realize that the Lord wants to go with them through their grief. Jesus is "a man of sorrows, and acquainted with grief; . . . He has borne our griefs and carried our sorrows; . . . He was wounded for our transgressions, he was bruised for our iniquities; upon Him was the chastisement that made us whole, and *with His stripes we are healed* (Isaiah 53:3–5 RSV, emphasis added). Jesus not only understands their grief, but he also is able to heal the pain of the grief.

Second, post-abortive women and men need to let other people help them work through their grief. A post-abortion support group should be a safe place for women and men to grieve their loss. Jane found that safety in a Conquerors group.

Jane's Story

Jane came to the Conquerors group twelve years after her abortion. Already feeling like a failure after a divorce, Jane had looked to Bill to cure her loneliness and relieve her feelings of rejection. After some months in this relationship, she became pregnant. Shaming herself for making this mistake, she and Bill decided she should have an abortion. A year and a half later she married Bill, but they agreed that they would *never* discuss the abortion again.

Turning her grief inward, she became depressed. She felt resentment toward her husband, but the protective walls they built around themselves to avoid the pain also shut out others who could have given support. Jane felt isolated.

Bill's decision after the abortion not to have anymore children further intensified her grief. Jane felt that not having another child with Bill only drove them further apart. It simply reinforced the disappointment and regret of having an abortion. Jane's three children from her first marriage became her only source of comfort. She became overly protective and derived her self-esteem from them.

A couple of years later, Jane became a Christian and specifically asked God's forgiveness for her abortion. But she did not experience healing at that time. Jane tried working with children and the pro-life movement, perhaps subconsciously trying to appease the guilt and shame she had from the abortion, yet she still had no peace. When she joined the Conquerors post-abortion group, she realized the importance of grieving the loss of her child instead of repressing her feelings.

Jane had a joyful expectancy of what God would do for her as she obediently submitted to him in true repentance. But she still felt apprehensive about the pain she would encounter in the process—pain she had been trying to avoid for years.

After much prayer, she felt the Lord telling her that her aborted child had been a boy. Able to identify him as a son, she felt set free to grieve his death and communicate her love for him. She named her son and wrote him a letter telling him of her love and asking his forgiveness. She also told him she would always wear a small ring as a loving remembrance of him. Where there had been only feelings of death and sin, Jane now was able to feel joy and love.

The Lord also revealed to Jane that the refusal to discuss the abortion was destroying the unity in their marriage. As she was writing the letter to her child, she found forgiveness for the old resentments, and God gave her a new love for her husband. She asked Bill to read the letter, and as he read it, he too faced his grief over the loss of their child. Two days afterward, on their tenth wedding anniversary, Bill gave Jane a gold ring with two hearts and a small diamond in the middle. "This made us all one," Jane said. "We are both very thankful for the power and healing love of God. He has brought restoration and unity to our lives and marriage. We are set free from our grief to love each other and our child."

Jane's story illustrates Elisabeth Kubler-Ross's five-stage grieving process: denial and isolation, depression, anger, bargaining, and acceptance.[1] Not all of these stages occur in an orderly sequence. Stages can and do happen together, and any or all of them can recur.

Stage One: Denial and Isolation

During the twelve years after Jane and Bill had their abortion, they felt isolated because they couldn't share their abortion experience, even with each other. They feared the church's response if they told them and even felt they couldn't talk to God about it. As Jane became more involved in the pro-life movement, the isolation became unbearable.

Another post-abortive woman says, "When you surround yourself with people who are always talking about the murder of the unborn and the slaughter of the innocents, you hardly feel at liberty to say you've had an abortion."

In the Conquerors group, Jane began to share some of these feelings with other women who understood. Her feelings of isolation lessened, and she broke through some of the denial of her abortion experience.

Denial is usually one of the first reactions women and men have over the loss of their child through abortion. They may deny that it is a baby they have aborted. They may deny that they had a choice—someone else coerced them into having an abortion. They may deny that the abortion has affected them emotionally or spiritually.

Just as our bodies react to physical pain by going into shock, our emotional and mental pain can cause similar reactions. Post-abortive women and men may react by becoming numb. Their emotions often become short-circuited and they experience mental blocks because they aren't ready to deal with their emotions.

Since Jane and Bill had agreed not to discuss the abortion experience with each other, they needed a lot of courage to face the pain they had been denying. They needed to admit that they had aborted a child, not just a piece of tissue.

Jane asked God to help her get in touch with her grief feelings, but she found difficulty in grieving the loss of her child because she didn't have any external evidence that he had ever existed. She had never seen him or held him. There had been no formal funeral service where others acknowledged he had lived or where she could grieve and get support. She and her husband were the only two who knew the child existed, and they had vowed not to talk about it. The guilt and shame they felt from voluntarily taking the life of their child only encouraged their denial.

Lyle, whose story we read in chapter 10, found that grieving the loss of his child was the most difficult thing to do in the healing process. He wonders now what his fourteen-year-old would look like, what talents he or she would have. He grieves because he will never know.

Stage Two: Depression

It is common for women and men who have had an abortion to be depressed. Jane experienced depression as well. Before she started dealing with her denial, she had repressing her feelings about the loss of her baby. This set the stage for her isolation and alienation from those she cared about, and she became depressed.

Jane did not fully realize why she was depressed. She felt a lack of self-esteem, numbness, sadness, hopelessness. Like many post-abortive women and men, she wanted to give up. This despondency can often lead to suicidal thoughts or abuse of alcohol, drugs, or food. Of course this only adds to the depression.

Joe, whose story we read in chapter 10, became so depressed when Betty told him she was having an abortion that he couldn't even sleep. After the abortion, he became even more depressed. He felt completely helpless and hopeless during this time.

Stage Three: Anger

As post-abortive women and men break through their denial and realize that they have taken the life of their child, they often experience much pain. In order to avoid this pain, they may become very angry toward the people they feel are responsible for the abortion.

Psychologist Anne Speckhard explains the role of anger in the grieving process: "As long as anger which is directed at others can be kept alive, the woman avoids experiencing intense feelings of loss and her responsibility for its occurrence. Thus intense anger directed toward others who were involved in the abortion event frequently surfaces from the unconscious at the time when the woman begins to define her loss."[2] Speckhard goes on to say that before the anger is expressed on a conscious level, it will be displayed on an unconscious level. The rage may be directed toward parents, men, children, abortion providers, or pregnant women. When the anger surfaces and the post-abortive woman or man is able to express it as feelings of loss, then the rage will begin to subside.

Post-abortive women and men express their anger about the loss of their child in various ways. Some people express it overtly—everyone knows they are angry. Many times, though, the anger may take the form of blaming. Others, like Jane, hold on to their anger until it turns to resentment. Then they either turn it inward, which results in depression and other physical ailments, or they project it outward to others. Don projected his anger inward until he became very bitter and resentful toward himself and his wife Pat. All these forms of expressing anger are destructive and destroy self-esteem and relationships, producing further guilt.

As post-abortive women and men deal with their anger, they may be afraid to let go of it. They may want to make someone pay to avoid dealing with the pain altogether. The Bible clearly directs us to "get rid of all bitterness, rage and anger, brawling and slander, along with every form of malice. Be kind and compassionate to one another, forgiving each other, just as in Christ God forgave you" (Eph. 4:31–32).

Paul talks about the importance of forgiveness and love again in Colossians 3:13–15: "Bear with each other and forgive whatever grievances you may have against one another. Forgive as the Lord forgave you. And over all these virtues put on love, which binds them all together in perfect unity. Let the peace of Christ rule in your hearts, since as members of one body you were called to peace. And be thankful." Only as these women and men put their trust in Christ for his love and forgiveness will they be able to forgive and love others.

Stage Four: Bargaining with God

Post-abortive women and men, especially if they are Christians, may be afraid of God and his punishment for sin.

Fearing what God might do to them, they may try to appease God or make amends.

At first these efforts may not be conscious. Post-abortive women and men may live with vague fear and guilt and know that they somehow want to pay for what they've done. Bargaining may manifest itself in a variety of behaviors, as we saw in chapter 7: becoming pregnant with a "replacement child," becoming active in the pro-life movement or a crisis pregnancy ministry, or maintaining a vigorous schedule of service activities. While none of these behaviors is negative in itself, if it is done in an attempt to bargain with God, it is destructive.

Post-abortive women and men need to identify how they are trying to appease God or make amends through their "good works." Then they can rest in the truth of Ephesians 2:8–9: "For it is by grace you have been saved, through faith—and this not from yourselves, it is the gift of God—not by *works,* so that no one can boast" (emphasis added). If they can through faith in Christ receive this gift of grace, they will be free from their need to earn God's acceptance. They can rest in his mercy and forgiveness, confident that "if we confess our sins, he is faithful and just and will forgive us our sins and purify us from all unrighteousness" (1 John 1:9).

Stage Five: Acceptance

As post-abortive women and men try to come to a point of acceptance, they will need to move through a process. They will need to

1. Identify what the loss is.
2. Realize that the child is not coming back.
3. Accept that they are the mother or father of the aborted child.
4. Accept that they have taken the life of the child.

5. Accept that the child is with Jesus in heaven.
6. Accept that they can't appease their child's death through bargaining.
7. Resolve feelings of anger toward self and others.
8. Accept God's forgiveness for the abortion.
9. Forgive those who were involved in the abortion decision.

Jane's prayer, asking God for a confirmation about the gender of her aborted child, broke her denial and gave her a mother's love. God in his mercy answered her prayers. To further help her break her denial, she wrote a letter to her son, telling him of her love and her feelings of loss. Sharing that letter with her husband completely shattered the denial. Now that their silence had been broken and their resentments were forgiven, they could openly talk about their son, grieve for him, and acknowledge his importance in their family. The ring symbolized their renewed unity.

Several dynamics will help post-abortive women and men break through their denial and move toward acceptance. First, they need a safe place where they will feel cared for and accepted, no matter what they have done. The Conquerors support groups try to provide that kind of nonjudgmental, nonshaming atmosphere. Second, they need to hear the stories of other Christian women and men who have had abortion experiences. They will find both comfort and courage in learning how other women and men are working through the issues related to the abortion. Third, they need to reflect on the different physical, emotional, and spiritual symptoms that the abortion caused. Through studying the nine steps in a group context, they can have the group's help and support to work through their guilt, shame, anxiety, anger, and grief.

GUIDED EXPERIENCES

A post-abortion support group can lead women and men through several guided experiences that will help them come to terms with their grief and loss.

The most basic place to start is for post-abortive women and men to share the details of their abortion experiences. If they are reluctant to share, group leaders or counselors may want to ask questions that will help them open up about the physical and emotional aspects of the pregnancy and abortion. As post-abortive women and men share, they will begin to deal with the repressed, unspoken feelings about their abortion. As they work through their pain, the other group members can encourage and support them by listening empathetically.

Grief Work

The Conquerors groups have found that post-abortive women and men benefit from setting aside a period of time to intentionally grieve the death of the aborted child.[3] Before they begin, they should make arrangements for some time away from their job and other daily responsibilities.

Before beginning the grief work, post-abortive women and men should tell the people closest to them that they are going to spend a brief time working through a grief process and that they may feel unusually sad for that period of time. They can let their friends know that though they need support and love, their friends should not feel responsible for making them feel better. They may want to enlist several friends or support-group members to pray for them during the specific time of their grief work.

Visualizing. One very effective way of working through grief is to do some visualization. Find a quiet place where you can feel free to talk or cry without anyone else hearing you. Then close your eyes and visualize your child. Don't visualize a torn, broken fetus but a whole, beautiful child. If it will help you feel the situation more realistically, hold a doll in your arms. Name your child. Remember how Dave (chapter 10) imagined his aborted child sitting in a chair across from him and how he named her Amy.

Verbalizing. Talk to your child. Tell him or her how you feel. Talk about your love or your guilt or your remorse. Remember as you talk to your child that he or she is in a perfect state of peace and completion in the care of Jesus. Your child feels no pain, sadness, or anger toward you; your child is not judging you. Feel free to cry and sob if those feelings well up inside you.

Reconciliation with the Aborted Child

1. Write a letter to your child, expressing your feelings toward him or her.
2. Write a letter from your child expressing his or her feelings for you. Please remember that your child is with God and holds no resentment toward you (appendix B).
3. Write a letter to God, expressing your feelings of grief. Then commit the care of your child to him.
4. Write a letter from God to you, expressing his forgiveness and comfort to you as well as his care for your child.
5. Choose a special remembrance such as a ring, a pin, a candle, or newly planted tree to represent your child.

6. Write a poem, (appendix A) draw or paint a picture, or complete a sculpture to represent your child. (Use other creative options as you wish).
7. Write or say a dedication prayer or have a personal ceremony committing your child to God's care.

15

Taking Responsibility for the Loss of My Child

Step 5: I am willing to confess to God that I am accountable for the loss of my child. I will honestly examine my own motives and actions as well as those of other people who were involved in my abortion decision.

It's important for post-abortive women and men to accept their personal responsibility for taking the life of their aborted child. They must assume accountability for that death. Most women and men agree that they use many defense mechanisms to avoid facing the reality of their responsibility in the abortion experience. Only as they examine these defense mechanisms and decide to let them go can they face the truth. Although this too is a very painful step, it is essential to recovery and wholeness.

ACCOUNTABILITY

What do we mean by accountability for the abortion? An adaptation of a dictionary definition describes well the accountability of the person who is involved in the decision to abort a child. Accountability means to be "answerable, liable to pay or make good in case of loss [of child]; responsible for a trust [of a life]; liable to be called to account [for death of the child]; answerable to a superior [God]."[1]

Because all of the people involved in an abortion decision are accountable, are answerable to God for taking the life of a child, they must realize the responsibility they have. In order for them to "pay or make good in case of loss," they need to face a holy God and admit their sin to him as David did: "For I know my transgressions, and my sin is always before me. Against you, you only, have I sinned and done what is evil in your sight" (Ps. 51:3–4).

The loss of a child can never be repaid, but Jesus mercifully paid the price for each aborted child's death. Only he can forgive and provide pardon for the loss. Those responsible need to come to Christ with a humble, penitent, broken heart and cry out as David did in Psalm 51:1–2: "Have mercy on me, O God, according to your unfailing love; according to your great compassion blot out my transgressions. Wash away all my iniquity and cleanse me from my sin."

Who Is Accountable for the Abortion?

Who is responsible for the death of the aborted child? Our society tends to point the finger at the woman in whose body the aborted child grew. They say, "She's responsible. It was her child." But is she the only one responsible? What about the parents who coerce their teenage daughter into having an abortion? Certainly they are accountable. And what about the husband or boyfriend who couldn't face the pregnancy? He too is accountable. And what about people who tell a woman that abortion is simply removing unwanted tissue (not a baby) and counsel her to have an abortion: friends, medical personnel, pregnancy counselors, school counselors, or pastors. They are accountable too.

But it doesn't do any good to push the blame on others. God knows the whole situation and holds us responsible. When we sin, we somehow hope we can hide it from God. We may be able to hide an abortion experience from friends, family, and the church; but we can't hide it from God. David knew this as well when he said: "O Lord, you have searched me and you know me. You know when I sit and when I rise; you perceive my thoughts from afar. You discern my going out and my lying down; you are familiar with all my ways. . . . Where can I go from your Spirit? Where can I flee from your presence? . . . Even the darkness will not be dark to you; the night will shine like the day, for darkness is as light to you" (Ps. 139:1–3, 7, 12). These verses are comforting for those who want to come to God and honestly face what they have done. But those who are trying to hide their sins from God may tremble.

Each person involved in the abortion has to admit to God that he or she is responsible for taking the life of a child. Because many post-abortive women or men are filled with guilt and shame, they sometimes take all the responsibility. Other women or men hold on to their anger and resentment toward others involved in the abortion decision and don't face their responsibility to God.

HINDRANCES TO RESPONSIBILITY

Some women or men are hindered from facing their responsibility for the abortion because they are afraid to face the pain. They feel that if they don't acknowledge their pain, they don't need to deal with it. They will do everything they can to protect themselves from feeling physical and emotional pain. Admitting that they have taken the life of a child is too painful for them to bear. Often they have committed other sins as well, and to face all that they have done and become is overwhelming.

Instead of facing reality, they use behavior patterns that help them cope. Although many of these defense mechanisms are means of survival, others are unhealthy and will impede the healing process. Post-abortive women and men recognize they use the following defense mechanisms to deal with their abortions.[2]

1. Suppression or repression. Some post-abortive women and men decide they can't or won't deal with the abortion experience. They push their feelings about the abortion totally out of their consciousness, trying to convince themselves that they have no feelings about it. They avoid introspection and engage in activities that keep them from reflecting. They often don't realize that when they repress a bad feeling, they also may repress many good feelings such as parental instincts, tenderness, and vulnerability. They also don't realize that these repressed feelings may surface strongly at certain sounds, smells, and situations.

2. Rationalization. Many women and men use excuses to rationalize their abortion. "I had the abortion because it was the only (or best) thing I could do at the time," or "I did it for my other children." They need to come to the place where they can say, "I was under pressure, and I couldn't withstand it. I gave in."

3. Denial. Others completely deny that the experience ever happened to them. They may look to drugs or alcohol to help them deny their abortion.

4. Blaming. Still others place all the responsibility for the abortion on someone else. They may say, "The abortion was all my parents' [boyfriend's or girlfriend's] fault. They [he or she] made me do it." Or a man may say, "My wife [girlfriend] made the decision without my permission."

5. Compensatory atonement. Some post-abortive women and men may try to compensate for the loss of the aborted child. They try to atone for their guilt in various ways. They may become pregnant again, trying to replace the aborted child. Others compensate by becoming supermoms or superdads or by placing unreasonably high expectations on their other children. None of these "atonements" solve anything.

6. Reaction formation. Reaction formation is a psychological term that describes behavior that denies a certain reality by reacting strongly in an opposite direction. In post-abortive women and men, this behavior may express itself in fanatical activities, like jumping on the pro-abortion bandwagon and helping women receive abortions.

7. Projection. Some post-abortive women and men project toward others their feelings about their abortion experience. They may be angry with themselves about the abortion, but instead of admitting it they project or put their anger into another person.

8. Avoidance. This behavior avoids people or things— pregnant women, infants, medical personnel, physical exams—that may trigger any emotional recall of the abortion experience.

Post-abortive women and men need to identify what defense mechanisms they have used to cope with their abortion experience. They then must decide to behave in more healthy ways, in ways that will move them toward recovery.

As they are going through the process, they may also recognize defenses that their spouse or boyfriend/girlfriend, parents, abortion providers, and friends have used. Doing so may trigger angry feelings toward these people. For instance, Don blamed Pat for the abortion and projected his anger onto her (chapter 10). Only recently has he begun to take responsibility for getting Pat pregnant in an out-of-wedlock situation. He's also taking responsibility for going along with the first abortion.

WORK TOWARD RESOLUTION

As you get in touch with your responsibility for your abortion decision, try to work toward a resolution of your feelings about yourself and others. Use the following suggestions to help you face your accountability and move beyond fear and denial to acceptance.

1. Write out the circumstances involved in your decision to abort. List your fears, your motives, and your rationalizations. Be absolutely honest. Admit completely your part in the abortion.

2. Write a letter to God, expressing all the emotions you feel about your part in the abortion decision. Ask God to help you accept responsibility for the abortion, to help you receive his forgiveness and healing. Ask him to help you let go of the shaming messages you have been giving yourself and to replace these messages with true messages of his love, mercy, and forgiveness.

3. Make a list of the influence other people and

circumstances have had in your abortion decision. Take into account such factors as the crisis state in which you made the decision. Think about what messages you had been given: "Don't come home pregnant" or "If you get a girl pregnant, don't come home" or "It's only tissue. What's your problem?" or "You can't afford another child."

4. Write letters to the people who influenced you to have an abortion. Tell them how you feel about their part in the abortion. (You probably will not want to send these letters. They merely are a tool to help you work through the issue of responsibility. However, suggestion 6 may result in a letter that you actually send.)

5. Write a letter to God, expressing your emotions toward all those who were involved in the abortion and the death of your child. Ask God to help you gain understanding and healing from these hurts. This will help you release your feelings toward these people in a healthy way, knowing that God knows the thoughts and motives of all people.

6. If you wish to educate your abortion provider about the hurt the abortion has brought to your life, you may wish to send him or her a letter expressing your anger and hurt over his or her cooperation in the taking of your child's life.

GOD'S PROMISES

As post-abortive women and men face their accountability to God for taking the life of their child, God's promises will help the healing process.

> God is light; in him there is no darkness at all. If we claim to have fellowship with him yet walk in the darkness, we lie and do not live by the truth. But if we walk in the light, as he is in the light, we have fellowship with one another, and the blood of Jesus, his Son,

purifies us from all sin. If we claim to be without sin, we deceive ourselves and the truth is not in us. If we confess our sins, he is faithful and just and will forgive us our sins and purify us from all unrighteousness (1 John 1:5–9).

HOMEWORK QUESTIONS

1. How do you generally deal with responsibility and accountability? Do you tend to assume too much responsibility for events and problems, or do you assume too little?

2. In what way(s) do you feel responsible and accountable for your abortion?

3. How do you feel toward yourself?

4. How do you think God sees you?

5. What defense mechanisms do you use to overlook your responsibility for the loss of your child? What step can you take to change this behavior?

6. If other people were involved in your decision, what was their part?

7. How do you feel toward them?

8. How do you think God sees them?

16

Evaluating My Relationships

Step 6: I will examine how my abortion experience has affected my relationships. This will include the issues of communication, co-dependency, and sexuality.

After taking responsibility for the abortion decision, post-abortive women and men need to assess how their abortion experience has affected their relationships. If any negative patterns such as co-dependency, impaired communication, or sexual problems have been established, post-abortive women and men need to take steps to replace these unhealthy patterns with healthy ones.

ABORTION AFFECTS RELATIONSHIPS

Post-abortive women and men can't ignore the fact that abortion changes their relationships to people of the opposite sex, to their dating partner, to their spouse, and to their family members (their parents and their other children, if any).

Relationships Between Women and Men

Female-male relationships suffer after an abortion. In the Conquerors women's study, 57.4 percent admitted an inability to share their deep inner feelings with men, and 52.3 percent said they even had difficulty sharing their thoughts and emotions with men. A little over half of these women began showing an inability or difficulty in sharing with men after their abortion experience. Chapter 10 also indicated that many men felt their communication with their girlfriend or wife was deeply affected by the abortion experience.

Not only have women had a difficult time sharing with men, but 47.1 percent acknowledged negative and hurtful relationships to men, and 38 percent said this started after the abortion. It appears that women who have had abortions have chosen men who treat them negatively. But of a greater concern, having an abortion seems to make them choose even more harmful relationships.

Marriage Relationship

Abortion also affects the marriage relationship. The Conquerors women admitted that 38.2 percent of them had marital problems, and of these women, 92.3 percent stated that their marital problems started after they had an abortion. As we examine the marriages of men who have been involved in an abortion (chapters 5 and 10), we see the negative effect the abortion experience has on their relationships.

Post-abortive women and men need to identify what is affecting their marriage. Are they angry at their spouse because of the abortion? Are they angry at the aborted baby's father or mother and projecting that anger onto their spouse?

Whatever their issues are, they must bring them to the surface so they can be discussed and healed.

In their book *The Act of Marriage,* Tim and Beverly LaHaye talk about married love and how it can be restored.

> Love is not a whimsical vapor that comes and goes without rhyme or reason. It is a vital emotion that grows or dies in direct proportion to one's thinking pattern. If a person gripes and criticizes his [her] partner in his [her] mind, before long his [her] love will die. If, however, that negative mental habit is replaced by thanksgiving for the positive characteristics in a partner's life, love will blossom as surely as night follows day. . . . Love is the result of thinking wholesome thoughts about one's partner. . . . Many times we have seen love return to a marriage when one or both were willing to obey the principle, "In every thing give thanks: for this is the will of God in Christ Jesus concerning you" (1 Thess. 5:18).[1]

In the Conquerors women's study, 26.5 percent of the women also acknowledged struggling with sexual frigidity. Of these, 88.9 percent stated that their frigidity started after the abortion. Conquerors men also struggled with being impotent for a period of time after their wife had an abortion. This was especially true for the men who tried to stop the abortion. Tim and Beverly LaHaye talk about the effect of guilt, revenge, and resentment on frigidity:

> Guilt is a common cause of orgasmic malfunction. . . . Whether related to an attempted rape for which the unwilling victim feels guilty, or an ill-advised adulterous liaison experienced prior to marriage, or promiscuity before or after marriage, guilt is a cruel taskmaster that must be confronted spiritually. . . . Getting things

straightened out with God [relieves] their guilty consciences, [and their] orgasmic malfunction ceases.[2]

The LaHayes go on to say that "Revenge, bitterness,
resentment, and other forms of hostility are not only devastat-
ing to one's spiritual life, but sexually demotivating. That is
true whether the object of one's wrath is many miles from his
[her] bedroom or lying in the same bed."[3]

Post-abortive women or men may receive release from
frigidity as they release their guilt, resentment, or feelings of
revenge. They may recognize that they feel these things about
their spouse.

If anger and frustration increase in the marriage
relationship, it can lead to abuse. In our Conquerors study,
20.6 percent of the women acknowledged domestic abuse. Of
these women, 85.7 percent said that the abuse began after the
abortion. Dave, whose story we read in chapter 10, shared
that as the resentment and stress grew in his marriage
because of the abortion, he had violent outbursts.

An Abused Wife's Story

"My husband seemed like a white knight when I met
him: flowers, dinner, immediately wanting to marry me. The
demand for sex before marriage and after was a daily thing.
After marriage, he controlled what I said, did, thought, who I
could be with, for how long, how much money I could have.
He isolated me from my family and friends. He made me wait
up for him late at night so that he could have sex when he
came home from work. My response to this was total
confusion. I had no one to talk to. He constantly criticized
and made fun of everything I did. I began to fantasize about
having a child, someone I could love who would love me. I
subconsciously forgot to take the pill on time. By the time I

had missed my third period, I finally went to see a doctor. I was pregnant. Several days of bitter arguments and accusations ensued. On a cold Sunday morning, he gave me the ultimatum that I had to choose between him or the child. I left the house and cried and walked aimlessly for several miles. I have never been so alone in my life. I was scared. My only choice, I believed, was to return to him and have the abortion. He arranged for the abortion but refused to go with me. He told me I had to take care of my own mess. When I returned from having the abortion, he left for several days. When he returned and for the next sixteen years, he never let me forget that I had forced him to make that decision to abort. Our relationship deteriorated to the point that I left him. We are now in the process of a divorce."

Parenting

Abortion also affects the way women and men function as parents. Statistics from the Conquerors women's study indicate that post-abortive women had difficulty in their parenting experience: 32.4 percent lack patience with children; 29.4 percent are sometimes verbally or emotionally abusive with them; 20 percent acknowledged frequent anger with their children; 14.7 percent admitted feelings of unexplained rage toward their children; and 13.2 percent felt they overdiscipline their children physically.

Some post-abortive women struggled with being overprotective with their children (29.4 percent) while others—at the other end of the spectrum—realized they were overly permissive. Some women wanted their children to stay young (27.9 percent); some had unreasonably high expectations for their children (26.5 percent); and others had difficulty bonding with their children (14.7 percent).

These parenting concerns not only affect women, but

may also affect men who have been involved in abortion experiences. Their unresolved feelings will influence how they parent their children. Gary, whose story we read in chapter 10, felt his abortion experience caused him to be overly permissive with his son. He said, "I was there for his every need. I never let him cry. I spoiled the kid rotten."

When post-abortive women and men do not resolve their anger and rage toward themselves, others, and God, they often project that anger onto their children. Unresolved perfectionistic, performance-based behaviors will also affect their parenting. Their expectations will be too high, and the children, unable to meet their parents' standards, will become exasperated. Many times the parents' behavior sends messages to the children:

PARENTAL BEHAVIOR	SENDS A MESSAGE
Double standards say:	"Don't ever talk to me disrespectfully. But I'll say to you what I want. I'm your parent. I'll yell at you if I choose."
Disrespect for age says:	"I don't care how old you are, you are my child, and you will do what I say."
Keeping secrets says:	"You shouldn't have told your father that."
Overprotective behavior says:	"I don't want you to play with the other kids, you may get hurt."
Overpermissive behavior says:	"I don't care what you do. Do whatever you want. You can have anything you want."

These unwritten rules do not show respect for children, encourage them to share their feelings, encourage honesty, or help them develop healthy independence.

To evaluate the communication operating in their

families, post-abortive women and men must ask themselves the following questions:

- What can't we talk about in our family?

- Do we treat our children with respect and care?

- Do we have unrealistic expectations of our children?

- Are we overprotective or underprotective of our children?

- Are our feelings about the abortion affecting our parenting?

- Which rules are good and useful in our family?

- Which rules do we need to change?

As post-abortive women and men assess how their relationships have been affected by their abortion experience, they may realize that several destructive behavior patterns have been established. Some of the most common negative patterns are impaired communication, co-dependency, and sexual addiction.

CHANGING NEGATIVE BEHAVIOR

The first step to changing negative behavior is recognizing destructive patterns. Post-abortive women and men may need help from other people to identify negative behavior patterns. The support group can play an important role in making it safe for women and men to face their destructive behavior and to find the courage and strength to change it.

Impaired Communication

Many post-abortive women and men struggle in their communication with others. As women and men struggle to maintain the secret of their abortion, denying their feelings, they become more isolated, and their communication suffers.

Post-abortive women and men can evaluate their communication skills by asking themselves the following questions:

- Do I express my feelings or hide them?
- Do I use inflexible words like *never* and *always?*
- Do I use judgmental words like *should?*
- Do I use blaming phrases like *you always* or *you should?*
- Am I a good listener?
- Do I react to a person's words, or do I listen for the feelings underneath the words?
- Do other people feel safe to tell me their feelings, thoughts, and opinions, or are they afraid I'll just jump on them?

How can negative patterns of communication be broken? How can a person move from saying things like "You always do things wrong" or "You should have known better than to do that" or "Why don't you ever listen to me?" to saying things that affirm or encourage or facilitate understanding?

God's love in our hearts motivates us and helps us communicate honestly and fully. Communication based on love, respect, and honesty will satisfy and heal. It can help break down the walls between ourselves and others.

In healthy communications, words, facial expressions, body movements, and tone of voice all express the same message. People do not have to hide anything. They can be honest with their feelings. If they choose not to share their emotions with someone, they can be honest and say, "I don't feel like sharing with you right now." When they are angry, they don't have to pretend they are fine.

In healthy communication, people don't have to feel as if someone is going to blame them, put them down, attack them, or ignore their thoughts. Instead, they will feel accepted, loved, affirmed, and listened to. If they make mistakes, they simply say they are sorry. Their communication leaves the other person's self-esteem—as well as their own—intact.

Co-dependency

Many post-abortive women and men have been caught in co-dependent relationships, relationships in which they've lost their own identities and are inordinately dependent on other people for a sense of self-worth. Not knowing how to establish appropriate personal boundaries, they can't tell where they start as an individual and where their relationship to another person begins.

These women or men are not able to make their own decisions, state their own opinions, or make wise decisions about their physical bodies. Some women feel that if someone tells them they should have an abortion, they have to do what they are told. Dave, whose story we read in chapter 10, was involved in a co-dependent relationship and felt he couldn't speak up when his wife wanted to have an abortion.

Jeff Van Vonderen says that this attempt to meet legitimate needs in illegitimate ways is idolatry. He defines idolatry as

> basing your sense of life, value, and acceptance on something other than God. Your view of yourself, your moods, and your sense of value depends on externals— that is, on people's opinion of you, on clothes, money, a

relationship, your behaviors (religious or otherwise). . . .
Idolatry is graven images and pagan rituals; but it is
also allowing what the neighbors think to control your
actions.[4]

Many post-abortive women and men have made idols
out of other people in their lives. They were so fearful of
losing the relationship that they were willing to sacrifice the
aborted child for the opportunity to hold on to the relationship. They felt they couldn't go on with their lives if the
relationship ended. Sadly, many times the relationship is
destroyed because of the abortion, and they lose the other
person anyway.

Many post-abortive women and men express their co-
dependency by totally giving themselves to the care of
another person. They gain self-esteem through their caretaking activity. In *Striking a Balance*, Veronica Ray talks about
the consequences of caretaking: "Caretaking is overresponsi-
bility, grandiosity, and self-righteousness. It's behavior based
on the belief that we should have all the answers for everyone
all the time. It's taking over, more than taking care. It's
running ourselves ragged to answer every need, real or
imagined, of others."[5] The author characterizes unhealthy
caretaking as behavior that

- takes care of every problem but our own.
- bases personal happiness on the happiness of others.
- develops unhealthy relationships: protecting, defend-
  ing, lying for others, and trying to control others.
- makes us feel used and victimized.[6]

Sexual Addiction

Some post-abortive women and men find they become
involved in increased sexual activity, sometimes to the point

that the sexual behavior becomes addictive. According to the Conquerors study, 18 percent of the women said that they had increased sexual activity after their abortion. They may have experienced a loss because of the abortion, and they tried to get pregnant again to fill this loss. Some women may be consciously aware of this; others may not be. In the Conquerors study, 13 percent acknowledged that they deliberately tried to get pregnant again to compensate for the child they lost.

In his story in chapter 10, Don shares how the abortion affected his sexual relationship to Pat. "The day after the abortion, Pat eagerly initiated oral sex with me. She probably was trying to pay me back in a compensatory fashion due to the fact that she forced my part in the abortion. After the two-week period of abstinence, she seemed to be sexually aroused and wanted sex all the time. Although she had much sexual desire, she was very paranoid about becoming pregnant again. I was interested in sex, but my mind was an emotional battleground, and for months after the abortion, I was impotent. During sex my mind would wander and become preoccupied with abortion. I would think about the abortionist, his tools, and the path he took to get his job done. I would think about how having sex was what made my dead baby in the first place."

Some women and men who have had abortion experiences are struggling with sexual addiction in their relationships. They become preoccupied and compulsive in their behavior and obsessive in their thoughts about sexual activity. Such activities could include masturbation, compulsive sexual activity of a heterosexual or homosexual nature, pornography, sometimes progressing to illegal sexual activity. These people are caught in a vicious cycle that brings shame, disgust, and damaged relationships.

Melvin had been in sexual relationships with more than one hundred women over a fifteen-year period. At least two of these relationships ended with an abortion. After many years, he has finally identified that he has a sexual addiction problem. Melvin did have one long-term relationship to a woman but subsequently found out that she, too, had a sexual addiction problem. While he remained faithful to this one relationship, she usually was dating three or four men at one time. When she became pregnant, Melvin felt the child was his, and he wanted her to marry him and keep the baby, but she refused. She had an abortion and ran off and married another man, but that marriage didn't last. She came back to Melvin, and they continued in this unhealthy relationship. For years he kept trying to get a commitment from her, but she seemed incapable of making one.

When Melvin committed his life to Christ, he became convicted about his lifestyle. He was filled with guilt and shame, repulsed by his addictive behavior and the abortions he was responsible for. God is now helping him to remain free of the sexual addictions that held him in their grip for so long.

LOVE, THE BASE OF ALL RELATIONSHIPS

Many post-abortive women and men were looking for love in their relationships. But they didn't know what true love was. They thought love was fulfillment and satisfaction. The love they found was romantic, passionate, self-centered, and non-committed. For them, it resulted in abortion, pain, and regret.

What is true, enduring love? True love is "patient [and] kind. It does not envy, it does not boast, it is not proud. It is not rude, it is not self-seeking, it is not easily angered, it keeps no record of wrongs. Love does not delight in evil but rejoices with the truth. It always protects, always trusts, always hopes, always perseveres. Love never fails" (1 Cor. 13:4–8). Isn't that a wonderful kind of love? Isn't it what we are all looking for?

Many post-abortive women and men look at the description in 1 Corinthians 13 and realize that their relationships have been *full* of rudeness, self-seeking, and anger. They and their partners carried with them long lists of recorded wrongs. Their love exposed each other, not protected each other. They rarely trusted each other. They frequently failed each other.

The kind of love described in 1 Corinthians 13 comes only when Christ's love permeates our hearts through a living relationship to him. Only he can give us the love that builds enduring relationships. And only he can give us love to rebuild our relationships that have been damaged by abortion.

HOMEWORK QUESTIONS

1. How has your abortion affected your relationship to others (spouse, male friends, female friends, children, relatives, others) in the past?

2. In what ways does your abortion experience affect your current relationships to others?

3. How have your underlying feelings about the abortion affected your communication with others?

4. What does the word *dependency* mean to you?

5. Complete the following sentences: (a) I feel overly dependent on others when . . . (b) I fear dependency on others when . . .

6. How has your abortion affected your sexuality?

7. What changes would you like to see occur in your relationships? Are you willing to commit yourself to these changes?

8. What do you need to do for these changes to take place?

17

Forgiving Myself

Step 7: I accept responsibility for the loss of my aborted child, and I will accept God's forgiveness and choose to forgive myself and others.

FORGIVENESS

Forgiveness is one of the more difficult issues for women and men who have had abortions. They are vulnerable because of their guilt and pain from past wrong choices. When post-abortive women and men can't forgive themselves or others, their feelings often turn to resentment. Forgiveness is a path that leads from the bondage of resentment to the freedom of peace.

Forgiving Ourselves

Some post-abortive women and men feel that abortion is the worst sin they could commit because they have taken the life of their own totally innocent child. They may even feel this is an unpardonable sin. These women and men can find great comfort in learning that God in his great love says, "'Come now, let us reason together,' says the Lord. 'Though your sins are like scarlet, they shall be as white as snow; though they are red like crimson, they shall be like wool'" (Isa. 1:18).

One of the most important facts about God's forgiveness is that he gives it to us. We can do nothing to earn or deserve his forgiveness. He gives it to us because he loves us and because Jesus paid the price for our guilt. "He was pierced for our transgressions, he was crushed for our iniquities; the punishment that brought us peace was upon him, and by his wounds we are healed" (Isa. 53:5).

In order to accept God's forgiveness and forgive ourselves, we need to see ourselves as sinful, imperfect people. If we are bound up in perfectionism and achievement, we will feel we are not good enough to be forgiven. We will continually strive to do better in order to be acceptable to God.

Furthermore, in order to experience God's forgiveness, we need to take seriously our responsibility to forgive others. Matthew 6:14–15 is a strong biblical directive that describes the relationship between God's forgiveness of us and our willingness to forgive others: "If you forgive men when they sin against you, your heavenly Father will also forgive you. But if you do not forgive men their sins, your Father will not forgive your sins."

This verse shows the importance that God places on forgiveness. In his ultimate wisdom, he knows that if women and men hold on to their feelings of resentment toward others, they may have difficulty receiving God's forgiveness. Refusing to forgive others hinders their fellowship with him. He understands that their harbored resentments will prevent them from being emotionally and spiritually healed and from enjoying fellowship with him.

Forgiving Others

As we've said in several previous chapters, post-abortive women and men are often angry with many people. They want to blame these other people for their pain and anguish. Part of resolving anger, part of grieving, part of taking responsibility for the death of their child involves forgiving these people who have hurt them.

At first, post-abortive women and men may feel justified in not forgiving these people. After all, these people may have pushed them into an abortion, or they may have rejected them after the abortion. Post-abortive women and men may think it isn't fair that they have to forgive when the other person should be asking them for forgiveness. They may rationalize that forgiving will excuse what the other person did. Joe was so angry with Betty because she wouldn't admit that the abortion was wrong. He continued to hold on to anger and resentment toward her until he saw that God's forgiveness was the only way to be released from the burden he had been carrying for years (chapter 10). Forgiving is not excusing what the other person has done but turning this person's accountability over to God and letting him hold him or her accountable.

Most post-abortive women and men find that forgiving other people who have harmed them is very hard work. They need to realize that they don't have the authority to judge others. Only God has that power. They need to come to the end of themselves and say, "I can't forgive, but God can empower me to forgive."

Forgiveness is not an option. It's a directive. The New Testament many times instructs us to forgive others. And forgiveness is not a "do-it-once-and-it's-done" experience. When the disciple Peter asked Jesus, "'Lord, how many times shall I forgive my brother when he sins against me? Up to seven times?' Jesus answered, 'I tell you, not seven times, but seventy-seven times'" (Matt. 18:21–22). Jesus wasn't talking about numbers or a legalistic system of forgiveness in this passage. He was talking about a person's heart condition. Post-abortive women and men are not to focus on how many times they forgive a person. They are to be willing to forgive, no matter how many times they have been wronged or will be wronged in the future.

Many times post-abortive women and men don't forgive the other person because they don't *feel* like forgiving. Forgiveness is an act of the will; it is not based on feelings. We can't wait to forgive until we feel like it. By faith, we need to forgive even if it doesn't make us feel any better. Matthew 18:35 speaks of forgiving from the heart. Only God can help us do that. As we ask God to give us a forgiving heart and stand on his promises to help us forgive, the feelings will come later.

When we are struggling to forgive others, we must understand that forgiveness changes the heart of the forgiver, not necessarily the forgiven one. Forgiving the other person is not an instant cure-all. The broken relationship may not be healed. But the forgiver's heart will never be the same. Post-abortive women and men may want to pray for the people they have resentment toward. They will find it hard to hold on to resentments against people for whom they are praying.

Sometimes we forgive people and later feel angry with them again about the old offense. Then we think that we must not have forgiven if we still have angry feelings. But certain things will naturally trigger those thoughts. At this point we need to stand on the Scripture verses that promise forgiveness, and we will find this anger having less and less control over us.

And remember, *forgiving is not the same as forgetting.* The trauma of an abortion is a wound that may leave its scar. Post-abortive women and men may never be able to *forget* their experience or those who hurt them. Some people say, "If you forgive me, you'll forget what I did." This isn't realistic. God is the only one who can forgive and forget. When they find the old anger returning, post-abortive women and men must practice continual forgiveness, making it a daily choice.

THE PROCESS OF FORGIVENESS

1. Acknowledge the need to be forgiven and to forgive others. Squarely face the reality that you need God's forgiveness and that you may need to forgive others.

2. Acknowledge the specific sins and people that need forgiveness. Ask God to show you the sins for which you need forgiveness and the specific people whom you need to forgive. Make a list of your offenses and the people to whom they are directed. If your list is long, start with the ones that are the most prominent and painful.

3. Ask God to forgive you. Read and memorize Scripture verses that affirm the importance of forgiveness. Go to a quiet place and ask God to forgive you for your part in the death of your child. Read him your list of other sins that you need him to forgive, and trust his promises to forgive you. If you have doubts in the future as to whether or not you are really forgiven, you can look back to this specific time and affirm, "I asked the Lord's forgiveness, and he forgave me on this particular date. This business is taken care of. I know I am forgiven."

4. Be willing to forgive. As previously discussed, many post-abortive women and men feel justified in not forgiving. You may need to ask God to give you a heart that is willing to forgive.

5. Release painful feelings. Many of these feelings may have been repressed for years, and getting in touch with them may be stressful. Verbally sharing feelings is an important tool in expressing them. You can do this in prayer or with a counselor or with a support group.

You may find it helpful to write a letter to the people whom you need to forgive. This process may help you get in touch with the pain that needs to surface so you can forgive. These letters do not have to be sent but are tools to release feelings and facilitate the process of forgiveness. Write as many letters as you need. You also may find it helpful to read your letters aloud to your support group or to a counselor.

Another way to help you release feelings of resentment toward another person is to imagine that the person is sitting in a chair across from you. Tell the person how she or he has hurt you. Express your resentments toward that person. Say aloud to the imaginary person, "I forgive you [name], for what you have done. I forgive you in Jesus' name."

If you feel that it would be helpful to both of you, arrange to meet with the person whom you need to forgive and tell that person that you forgive her or him. Be sure your motive is to offer healing forgiveness and not to rehash hurts and conflict. Whether or not you do this depends on the individual person and the individual relationship. You may want to have support-group members or a counselor help you assess whether or not a face-to-face meeting would be beneficial. If the person is someone you live with or someone who is very close to you, a face-to-face meeting may be important. If you are fearful of the response, you may want to have a counselor or pastor sit in on the meeting.

6. Ask God to forgive the people you resent. **Pray, asking God** to forgive the people whom you need to forgive. Then ask him to help you forgive them. You may find it helpful to come to God with a list of people you need to forgive and ask him to help you forgive these people one by one.

HOMEWORK QUESTIONS

1. What does forgiveness mean to you?

2. What part does forgiveness play in the healing process?

3. Are you able to forgive yourself? If not, why not?

4. If you have not taken the six concrete steps in the process of forgiveness, take time to do them now.

5. Based on your understanding of God's character and his promises in the Bible, write a letter from God to you, expressing his forgiveness of you and his love for you personally.

6. Whom do you need to forgive?

7. How do you feel about forgiving those who have hurt you?

8. Is there anyone from whom you need to seek forgiveness?

18

Improving My Self-Image

Step 8: I acknowledge that I am a special person. I am important to God. With his help, I will develop a positive self-image and work toward my full potential.

WHAT IS SELF-ESTEEM?

Self-esteem is what we think about ourselves, how we see ourselves. Proverbs 23:7 says, "For as he thinks in his heart, so *is* he" (NKJV). What post-abortive women and men say to themselves is what they believe they are. This self-perception will affect how they relate to others and God.

HOW DO WE DEVELOP SELF-ESTEEM?

How do we develop our self-image? We see ourselves through the eyes of our family, through our own perceptions, through the eyes of other people around us, and through the eyes of God.

The self-concept of the women and men who have had an abortion may be greatly affected by what has happened in their families. Did their parents and other family members treat them with unconditional love? Did their parents show respect toward them? What messages did they receive from their family as they were growing up? What crisis events in their childhood or adolescence may have caused trauma? The culmination of these events affects how these women and men see themselves today. Dave's self-esteem was deeply affected by the lack of love and nurturing from his parents. His self-esteem was even more destroyed when he became a victim of sexual abuse (chapter 10).

The self-esteem of post-abortive women and men is also affected by what they think about themselves. What do they say in their heart about themselves? What are their emotional, spiritual, and physical self-concepts? They may see themselves as physically unattractive. Their emotions may tell them that they are terrible people because they took the life of their child. They may see themselves as having failed spiritually by a making a decision that goes against God's commandments.

Other times, post-abortive women and men try to find their self-esteem in others. They may look to others' opinions, praise, or criticism of them. They may see themselves as undesirable because someone told them they were ugly.

The fourth source of our self-concept is God—seeing ourselves as God sees us. In his book *His Image, My Image,* Josh McDowell says, "A healthy self-image means having a realistic view of ourselves from God's perspective, as we are portrayed in His Word. I add the phrase 'no more and no less' because some people have an inflated view of themselves (pride), while others have a self-deprecating view of themselves (false humility)."[1]

HOW DOES GOD SEE YOU?

God sees you as a special creation that he made, and he has given you special tasks to do. The psalmist asks the question, "What is man that you are mindful of him, the son of man that you care for him?" Then he proclaims, "You made him [man/woman] a little lower than the heavenly beings, and crowned him with glory and honor. You made him ruler over the works of your hands; you put everything under his feet" (Ps. 8:4–5). God has a plan for the women and men who have had an abortion. He has a work for them to do.

God also sees you as special creations for whom he wants to provide protection and direction. Psalm 91:11–12 says, "For he will command his angels concerning you to guard you in all your ways; they will lift you up in their hands, so that you will not strike your foot against a stone." As post-abortive women and men struggle to deal with their pain about the abortion, God will "lift them up."

Finally, Psalm 139:13–14 describes the specialness of each life that God creates: "For you created my inmost being; you knit me together in my mother's womb. I praise you because I am fearfully and wonderfully made; your works are wonderful." Each life is "wonderful," including the life of post-abortive women and men as well as the life of the aborted child. Each wonderful creation has much worth because God has knit it together by his own hands.

HOW DO YOU SEE YOURSELF?

If God loves you, then you should love yourself. Right? But many people feel that if they are going to be good Christians, they should not love themselves. Instead, they feel they should belittle themselves. They call this humility.

The Bible says, "Love the Lord your God with all your heart," but it also says, "Love your neighbor as yourself" (Mark 12:30–31). The order seems to be: love God first, love yourself second, and love your neighbor third. Scripture tells us that God is our source of love, and as we love him, we can also love ourselves. This self-love, then, gives us the resources to love others. Self-love can also be called self-esteem, which is our foundation for loving others.

Some people would say that Romans 12:3 argues against self-love. It says, "I say to every one of you: Do not think of yourself more highly than you ought." Paul does not want us to be proud and think more of ourselves than God intended, but he does want us to see ourselves realistically as God sees us.

Paul talks about self-love in Ephesians 5:28–29. He says, "He who loves his wife loves himself. After all, no one ever hated his own body, but he feeds and cares for it, just as Christ does the church." The goal, then, of post-abortive women and men should be to develop this positive self-love or self-esteem.

Donna's Story

Donna got pregnant when she was in the tenth grade. It was a traumatic event that deeply affected her self-esteem. Donna's mother wanted her to have an abortion because she was so young and immature. Donna went along with her mother's decision because she couldn't see any other alternative. She was afraid of what people would think if they knew she was pregnant, and she didn't know how she could afford to raise a child by herself. The baby's father couldn't help financially either.

Donna attended the Conquerors group to help work

through her feelings about the abortion. As she has applied the principles of step 8, "Improving My Self-Image," she has developed a more positive self-concept. With this new self-confidence, she is now helping other women who have had abortions. She shares what she has learned:

"Two things have helped my self-esteem to improve. One is the knowledge that I'm loved and important to God. He has made me as a special creation, and he has a special purpose for my life. The second is knowing that other things may change in my life, but God is always constant. Learning that my self-esteem does not depend on how others see me but only who I am in Christ has given me a lot of security. I have to make many choices every day. I have learned that I will never get anywhere in life if I make my choices on the basis of wanting to look good or feel good. I have learned to set goals in the areas I need to change in my life. If I'm going to change negative behaviors that are defeating me, goal setting is important. I'm learning how to make good choices in my life. The choice I made to have an abortion was not a good choice and has damaged my self-esteem. I know other women who had high self-esteem before they had an abortion but felt bad about themselves afterward. I'm still struggling with feeling down on myself for the abortion, but I have to remind myself that I'm okay and that God loves me. Not being able to share the abortion with the children I have now is difficult. I don't like to keep secrets from them. Sharing the abortion with other people is still difficult. I'm afraid they will look down on me. Helping other woman who have had an abortion does help me to feel as if my life is worthwhile."

DEVELOP A POSITIVE SELF-IMAGE

1. Make a list of all the gifts and talents God has given you. If you are having difficulty doing this, ask a close friend, group leader, or pastor to help you. Then start praising and thanking God for the gifts and talents he has given you. Take action and use your gifts. For example, if you have a gift of teaching, ask to teach a Sunday school class. If your gift is singing, join the choir or offer to use your voice in another way for God's glory. If you have the gift of encouragement, send notes to people who need to be lifted up.

2. Ask people close to you what they like about you. This exercise can be very affirming. Internalize what they tell you, and again praise God for your specialness. When others give you compliments for doing something well, say, "Thank you." Don't belittle yourself and say, "I should have done a better job." Tell yourself, "I did the best I could." Don't dwell on the negative messages, but replace them with positive messages about the good qualities God has given you or with Scripture verses that affirm your self-worth.

3. Allow yourself to make mistakes. If you are putting yourself down because you have made a mistake, say to yourself, "It's okay for me to make mistakes. I'm not perfect, and God doesn't expect me to be perfect. With God's help I'll try to do better next time." If other people are upset with you because you have made a mistake, say to yourself, "I can understand why they are angry with me, but my self-esteem does not depend on their liking me. I'll apologize and will try to do better next time."

4. Take a look at the choices you make. Are they adding to your low self-esteem? Are you living in some sin that makes you feel bad about yourself and guilty before God? If so, let go of that sin. If you are involved in an unhealthy dependent relationship, get help from a support group or other friends to let go of it.

5. *Set goals.* List the behaviors that need to change in your life. Then write out a step-by-step plan explaining how you are going to change these behaviors. You can even set up for yourself a reward system for small achievements. Work on only one or two behaviors at a time. Don't give up and become discouraged if you fail. Regroup and start again. It has taken you years to develop these behaviors; it may take years to overcome them.

6. *Find forgiveness.* If the guilt surrounding your abortion is affecting your self-esteem, share these feelings in the group or with a counselor. Seek forgiveness from God for the sin of your abortion. If God has forgiven you, his special creation, who are you to refuse that forgiveness?

7. *Trust God.* If you are struggling with trusting God for who you are in him, go back to chapter 8 and read again the information about distorted images of God. Look at the Scripture verses that describe who he is, his love, and his acceptance of you.

HOMEWORK QUESTIONS

1. Complete the following sentences with how you see yourself:

I am _____

I am _____

I am _____

I am _____

2. What do I do (performance) to get people to look at me as a "somebody"—a person of value and worth?

3. In what ways do I try to *earn* the acceptance and love of God and others?

4. What do I do (protection) to keep people from seeing who I am?

5. Read the following Scripture passages and ask yourself, How do I feel when I read these? Am I beginning to value myself the way God values me?
   Isaiah 54:10
   Jeremiah 31:3
   Romans 5:7–8; 8:37
   Ephesians 1:4, 18
   Philippians 4:19
   1 John 3:1

19

Continuing My Healing Process

Step 9: I acknowledge God's sovereignty and will strive to learn his plan for my life. I will choose to continue the process of healing from my abortion, and I will use my experience to encourage others and help bring restoration into their lives.

The continuing healing process for post-abortive women and men can be approached in three steps: find and follow God's plan, continue the recovery process, and serve others.

FIND AND FOLLOW GOD'S PLAN

Put God First

The first step in finding God's plan is putting him first. Matthew 6:33 says, "Seek first his kingdom and his righteousness, and all these things will be given to you as well." Nothing else can come before Christ—not family, friends, work, or anything else. God wants total commitment and devotion.

233

Living a righteous, holy, and pure life is the second thing God requires of women and men who are recovering from abortion experiences. God asks them to be willing to let go of any known sin and to keep his commandments. Ecclesiastes 12:13 says, "Fear God and keep his commandments; for this is the whole duty of man [and woman]."

Trust God for Direction

As post-abortive women and men seek to find God's direction, they must trust him for insight. Proverbs 3:5–6 says, "Trust in the Lord with all your heart, and do not rely on your own insight. In all your ways acknowledge him, and he will make straight your paths" (RSV). God may want them to get out of an unhealthy relationship, reconsider their vocational direction, or develop more nurturing parenting skills. When unsure of what direction to take, repeating this verse as a prayer will help pinpoint their need to trust him.

Memorize and Meditate on God's Word

Women and men who have guilt and shame about their abortion experience need to meditate on Scripture passages that apply God's truth to their lives. Colossians 3:16 says, "Let the word of Christ dwell in you richly," and the Bible speaks of the special blessing for the person whose "delight is in the law of the Lord [on which she or he] meditates day and night" (Ps. 1:2). This delight comes only as we open our minds to God's Spirit and spend time in the Scriptures, asking him to illuminate them for us. God often reveals his will to us as we saturate our minds with his Word.

Memorizing Scripture allows people to have God's Word available in the forefront of their minds for whenever they need it. God says, "You shall therefore lay up these words of mine in your heart and in your soul; and you shall bind them as a sign upon your hand, and they shall be as frontlets between your eyes" (Deut. 11:18 RSV). The concept of the frontlets represents the importance of God's Word—as if it were tied onto our foreheads, between our eyes. When post-abortive women and men awake at night with some disturbing thought about the abortion, God's Word is powerful in bringing peace and comfort.

A reservoir of Scripture can also be a forceful deterrent to sin. David said, "How can a young man [or woman] keep his [or her] way pure? By living according to your word. . . . I have hidden your word in my heart that I might not sin against you" (Ps. 119:9–11).

Pray

Paul said, "Pray in the Spirit on all occasions with all kinds of prayers and requests" (Eph. 6:18). Post-abortive women and men can discover what God expects of them when they spend time in prayer. As they admit they're powerless without him and admit their need, he will hear their prayers and answer them. He may not always answer in the way they expect because he sees our life situations from his divine perspective. He says, "'My thoughts are not your thoughts, neither are your ways my ways,' declares the Lord" (Isa. 55:8). But he does promise to answer. He says, "Call to me and I will answer you and tell you great and unsearchable things you do not know" (Jer. 33:3).

Praise God

God "inhabits the praise of his people." He wants post-abortive women and men to echo the psalmist's pledge: "I will extol the Lord at all times; his praise will always be on my lips" (Ps. 34:1). When they praise God for the difficult circumstances of their abortion and other crises in their life, they are admitting that all these things are in his control. Praising releases God's power to work in the situation.

When post-abortive women and men feel discouraged, they will find that praising God for all the good things he has done for them can lift their spirits and help them refocus on him. David was a master at this: "Praise the Lord, O my soul, and forget not all his benefits—who forgives all your sins and heals all your diseases, who redeems your life from the pit and crowns you with love and compassion" (Ps. 103:2–4).

Withstand Satan's Attacks

The Bible speaks of Satan lying in wait, trying to destroy those who are trying to live for God. Peter says, "Be self-controlled and alert. Your enemy the devil prowls around like a roaring lion looking for someone to devour" (1 Peter 5:8). Women and men involved in abortion experiences have been deceived by Satan, and they will need to stand against him: "Be strong in the Lord and in his mighty power. Put on the full armor of God so that you can take your stand against the devil's schemes" (Eph. 6:10–11).

Satan is the author of lies and deception. He has deceived women and men into thinking that what they want to do—their own selfish goals or excuses—is more important than what God wants them to do. They often believe his lie that says they are not taking the life of a child.

If they want to live for God and do his will, they will need to pray for God's armament against Satan's attacks. Ephesians 6:13–18 lists the armor that God provides:

> Use every piece of God's armor to resist the enemy whenever he attacks, and when it is all over, you will still be standing up. But to do this, you will need the

strong belt of truth and the breastplate of God's approval. Wear shoes that are able to speed you on as you preach the Good News of peace with God. In every battle you will need faith as your shield to stop the fiery arrows aimed at you by Satan. And you will need the helmet of salvation and the sword of the Spirit—which is the Word of God. Pray all the time (TLB).

The best way of defeating Satan's lies is with the *belt of God's truth* holding us together. Post-abortive women and men especially need God's protection for their hearts—the center of their emotions and source of their self-worth. That's why they need the *breastplate of God's approval* for protection. The *shoes* God provides help them to walk in his way and pass along the good news of peace with God through salvation. The *shield of faith* protects them from Satan's fiery arrows.

The *Life Application Bible* explains it this way: "What we see are Satan's attacks in the form of insults, setbacks, and temptations. But the shield of faith protects us from Satan's flaming arrows. With God's perspective, we can see beyond our circumstances and know that ultimate victory is ours."[1]

Another of Satan's attacks is making post-abortive women and men doubt their salvation. The *helmet of salvation* protects their minds from doubting that God could save them because of what they have done. They can wield the *sword of the Spirit,* which is the Word of God, to take the offense in their battle against Satan's attacks. Once post-abortive women and men have been forgiven, Satan will try to get them to doubt that they really have forgiveness. They can use the Word of God to answer these lies.

In addition to putting on the armor, post-abortive women and men will need to learn to resist Satan when he comes to tempt them, quickly fleeing from the situation if necessary, to avoid yielding to sin. James says, "Submit yourselves, then, to God. Resist the devil, and he will flee from you" (James 4:7).

CONTINUE THE RECOVERY PROCESS

God's plan includes continued healing from the abortion experience. Paul says, "He who began a good work in you will carry it on to completion" (Phil. 1:6). Participation in the Conquerors nine-step recovery program may have helped post-abortive women and men resolve some of the pain that they have experienced from the abortion, but recovery is a lifelong journey. It's encouraging to know that they "can do everything through [Christ] who gives [them] strength" (Phil. 4:13).

Seek Freedom

The goal of post-abortive women and men is to come to the place where the abortion issues lose their power over them so that they are no longer incapacitated. As they trust God, they become free of the guilt and shame that has been binding them. "Where the Spirit of the Lord is, there is freedom" (2 Cor. 3:17).

At certain times, the feelings surrounding the abortion may come back to haunt them—the anniversary of the abortion or when they see a child of the same age. This may trigger their pain. During these times, they can find freedom and comfort in knowing God will be with them. He says, "Fear not, for I have redeemed you; I have summoned you by name; you are mine. When you pass through the waters, I will be with you; and when you pass through the rivers, they will not sweep over you. When you walk through the fire, you will not be burned; the flames will not set you ablaze" (Isa. 43:1–2).

Change Behavior

Part of the process of post-abortion recovery is to change old behaviors that inhibit growth. Paul says, "Put off your old nature which belongs to your former manner of life and is corrupt through deceitful lusts, and be renewed in the spirit of your minds, and put on the new nature, created after the likeness of God in true righteousness and holiness" (Eph. 4:22–24 RSV).

This putting off of the old behavior and renewal of the mind cannot be done in the post-abortive person's own strength. But it can take place as women and men by faith appropriate Christ's death on the cross and realize its power in their lives. Paul tells about this transaction in Galatians 2:20: "I have been crucified with Christ and I no longer live, but Christ lives in me. The life I live in the body, I live by faith in the Son of God, who loved me and gave himself for me."

Let Go, Let God

There comes a time in the recovery process when women and men who have had an abortion experience need to let go of the debilitating pain of the abortion and go on, with God's help, to experience a deeper Christian walk. Paul came to a similar place in his life. He said, "Forgetting what is behind and straining toward what is ahead, I press on toward the goal to win the prize for which God has called me heavenward in Christ Jesus" (Phil. 3:13–14).

Become Fruitful

Post-abortive women and men will always feel sadness when they think of the aborted baby. But as they express these feelings to the Lord and ask his Spirit to fill them, they will begin to experience the outgrowth of his presence in their lives: "love, joy, peace, patience, kindness, goodness, faithfulness, gentleness and self-control" (Gal. 5:22–23).

SERVE OTHERS

Many women and men who have found relief from their abortion pain want to help others who struggle from post-abortion trauma. Before they begin helping other people, they need to examine their motives and be sure that they are qualified beyond their own experience.

A pastor or a Conquerors leader will need to evaluate post-abortive women and men to determine whether they are emotionally or spiritually stable enough to help others. If they lack the requirements or if they are motivated by the wrong reason, then they may need more support and training from Christian leaders before they can effectively help others.

Negative Motives

Self-satisfaction. Sometimes post-abortive women and men want to help others because it makes them feel good about themselves. It makes them feel important. Instead of finding their self-esteem in Christ, they try to find it in caring for hurting people. This can cause a problem. If the people they are helping do not make progress, they may feel that they have failed, further damaging their self-esteem. They may put themselves down for not being able to help the other person.

Gaining approval. Other times their service may be the means of getting approval from others in the church or community. They think these people will notice them and look up to them for what they are doing. But when post-abortive women and men look to others for approval, they will be disillusioned and unfulfilled. A time will come when something goes wrong, and someone in the church or community will be disappointed in their service. Then the post-abortive women and men will feel they have failed everyone.

Healthy Motives

1. The desire to be the aroma of Christ. Paul says in 2 Corinthians 2:15–17, "We are to God the aroma of Christ among those who are being saved and those who are perishing. . . . Who is equal to such a task? . . . In Christ we speak before God with sincerity, like men [and women] sent from God." Recovering post-abortive women and men will want to give off the fragrance of Christ.

2. The desire to bear others' burdens. As Christ bore the sin and guilt on the cross of Calvary for all the world, so he asks post-abortive women and men to reach out in the name of Jesus and help others who have heavy loads of pain. Christ has asked them to "carry each other's burdens, and in this way fulfill the law of Christ" (Gal. 6:2).

3. The desire to comfort others. God has reached down to women and men in their post-abortive recovery and has shown compassion and care to them when they are hurting. "The Father of compassion and God of all comfort" is now asking them to reach out, giving others the comfort he has given to them "so that [they] can comfort those in any trouble with the comfort [they themselves] have received from God" (2 Cor. 1:3–4).

4. The desire to boast of God. Some of the women and men who have had abortion experiences may feel that God could never use them. They may feel they are not bright enough or talented enough or strong enough in their faith to be used in serving others. Because of their sin of abortion, they may feel inadequate. These people may find encouragement in 1 Corinthians 1:27–31: "God chose the foolish things of the world to shame the wise; God chose the weak things of the world to shame the strong. He chose the lowly things of this world and the despised things—and the things that are not—to nullify the things that are, so that no one may boast before him. It is because of him that you are in Christ Jesus. . . . 'Let him who boasts boast in the Lord.'"

QUALIFICATIONS

Not only must post-abortive women and men make sure their motives are healthy before they begin helping other post-abortive strugglers, but they also must be qualified through their personal growth, experience, and maturity. An effective helper will possess these qualities:

Objectivity. Post-abortive women and men will not be able to help hurting people if their own self-esteem is connected to the serving. They may take personally everything that the people they are helping project onto them. They may get angry with the people they are serving and end up hurting them instead of helping them.

Emotional stability. Sometimes it's difficult to evaluate what level of emotional health the post-abortive women and men need to be able to serve others. If their emotional problems are still very painful, it may be difficult to separate their pain from the pain of those they are helping. They may then give counsel out of their own unresolved issues instead of counsel that would benefit the person they are trying to help.

For example, if a post-abortive woman still has a lot of anger toward men, she may not be able to give help to another woman who is struggling with a similar problem.

Spiritual maturity. New Christians who have had abortion experiences may have a vital witness for Jesus Christ and may grasp quickly the truths of God's Word. They may be able to be effective spiritual helpers. Others may not have a mature understanding of how to use God's Word to give counsel to those who are hurting and need spiritual counseling.

Ability to resist temptation. Another concern in ministering to other people is found in Galatians 6:1: "If a someone is caught in a sin, you who are spiritual should restore him [or her] gently. But watch yourself, or you also may be tempted." It's important for post-abortive women and men to have an understanding of their personal weak areas—for example, co-dependency or sexual temptation—so that they won't fall into sin. If a woman or man is vulnerable in these areas, she or he may end up getting emotionally or sexually involved with the person being helped. While the helping person's motives may have been good, Satan used the post-abortive person's weakness to bring defeat and chaos.

If women and men who have had abortion experiences are caught in a sin that is incapacitating and if they are not willing or able to let go of that sin, they need to refrain from helping others. Galatians 5:19–21 tell of these sins: "Impure thoughts, eagerness for lustful pleasure, idolatry, spiritism (that is, encouraging the activity of demons), hatred and fighting, jealousy and anger, constant effort to get the best for yourself, complaints and criticisms, the feeling that everyone else is wrong except those in your own little group—and there will be wrong doctrine, envy, murder, drunkenness, wild parties, and all that sort of thing" (TLB). The ministry of helping others can't receive God's blessing when post-abortive women and men are caught in these sins. Some may say, "The sin of envy or anger isn't so bad. I should still be able to minister." But these sins are bad because they get in the way of the Holy Spirit using a person as a vessel for his service.

Called by God. Seeking God's will is the most important prerequisite of serving others in a post-abortive ministry. If it isn't God's plan for a woman or man to help others recover from post-abortion symptoms, that person should look for another area of service. Much prayer should go into making this important decision.

REFLECTIONS QUESTIONS

1. What areas have you grown in since you started the group 12 weeks ago?

2. What areas around your abortion experience still need healing?

3. Do you need to attend another 12-week session to receive help in these areas?

4. Has your relationship with God changed; if so, how?

Appendix A

A grieving woman who had aborted her son many years before came to the realization that her son was made in the image of God. She wrote a poem telling of her love for her son and of God's love and forgiveness of her.

THE SON

My child, my son of love,
What I would give to have you now;
To hold, to kiss, to caress your brow.
I did not want you then—long ago,
I was much younger, and I just did not know;
That every pregnancy is a gift of love,
made by God's own hand
with an image stamped from above.
Oh, God, your mercy—your unfathomable grace,
I bask in it, splash in it,
let it shine on my face;
Let it soak and seep into the depths of my soul,
and cleanse and heal that deep, wide hole.
You love me even though I murdered my son.
His blood cries out for vengeance to be done—
But you have forgiven because of your Son.

Appendix B

One woman who has had an abortion shares her feelings in a letter to her aborted daughter, Tamar. She wishes now that she would have placed Tamar for adoption instead of aborting her.

To my daughter Tamar,

I'm sorry for ending your precious life. Please forgive me for being selfish. I never gave you a chance to live and express your feelings to God, me, your dad, or anyone else. I'm sorry you suffered. I have suffered emotionally since the second I aborted you. For thirteen years I even denied you existed before I accepted the reality of what I had done to you.

The only way I have been able to cope with it is through the love and forgiveness of Jesus Christ. Jesus has healed some of my emotional problems I've suffered since aborting you.

Currently you have no sisters or brothers. You are my only child, but soon you'll have a brother or sister through adoption. I wish I would have given you up for adoption instead of thinking only about myself. Oh, how happy you would have made a couple like your father and me, to be blessed with a precious gift from God.

Your father and I picked your name from a story in the Bible, 2 Samuel 14:27. Tamar was the only daughter of

King David, and she was very beautiful. So since your father's name is David and since you are our only child right now, we decided to name you Tamar.

Tamar, I love you very much, and I'm looking forward to the moment we'll be united in heaven. For now I know you're in complete peace, and Jesus is holding you in his arms. Good-bye. I love you.

Love,
Your mom

Notes

Chapter 1: How Did We Get into This Mess?

1. John Kantner and Melvin Zelnick as quoted in Claudia Wallis's, "Children Having Children," *Time* (December 9, 1985): 81.
2. Jerry Johnston, *Going All the Way* (Waco, Tex.: Word Books, 1988), 102.
3. Ibid., 102–3.
4. Ibid., 103.
5. National Center for Health Statistics, *Redbook* (September 1987): 148.
6. Claudia Wallis, "Children Having Children," *Time* (December 9, 1985): 79–90.

Chapter 2: Where Has the Church Been?

1. Jeff Van Vonderen, *Tired of Trying to Measure Up* (Minneapolis: Bethany House, 1989), 65.
2. Ibid., 65–66.
3. Charles Colson, with Ellen Santilli Vaughn, "Living in the New Dark Ages," *Christianity Today* (October 20, 1989): 30.
4. Ibid., 30–31.
5. John Piper, *Desiring God* (Portland, Ore.: Multnomah, 1986), 19.
6. Curt Young, *The Least of These* (Chicago: Moody, 1983), 147.
7. Charles Colson, with Ellen Santilli Vaughn, "Living in the New Dark Ages," *Christianity Today* (October 20, 1989): 33.
8. Ibid., 32.
9. Curt Young, *The Least of These* (Chicago: Moody, 1983), 161.
10. Josh McDowell, *How to Help Your Child Say "No" to Sexual Pressure* (Dallas: Word, 1987), 100–101.

Chapter 3: Where Have All the Children Gone?

1. *Family Planning Perspectives,* a journal of the Alan Guttmacher

248

Institute, an affiliate of Planned Parenthood (January/February and March/April, 1987).

2. Pregnancy Epidemiology Br. and Research and Statistics Br., Div. of Reproductive Health, Center for Chronic Disease Prevention and Health Promotion, Centers for Disease Control.

3. John Piper, *Abortion: A Pastor's Perspective* (Minneapolis: Bethlehem Baptist Church, 1989), 4.

4. Donald Shoemaker, *Abortion, the Bible, and the Christian* (Cincinnati: Hayes Publishing Company, 1982), 19.

5. Gary Bergel, with C. Everett Koop, M.D., *When You Were Formed in Secret* (Reston, Va.: Intercessors for America, 1986), I-6.

6. Center for Chronic Disease Prevention and Health Promotion, Centers for Disease Control. Pregnancy Epidemiology Br. and Research Br., Div. of Reproductive Health, vol. 38, no. 38 (September 29, 1989).

7. Anne Hollister, "The Unborn Patient: Radical New Methods of Healing a Fetus," *Life* (April 1983): 39.

8. A. W. Liley, *The Human Life Bill*, Vol. 2, p. 32.

9. Bernard Nathanson, *Aborting America* (Garden City, N.Y.: Doubleday, 1979), 165.

10. James K. Hoffmeier, ed., *Abortion: A Christian Understanding and Response* (Grand Rapids: Baker, 1987), 169–70.

11. Larry and Diane Mayfield with Jerry B. Jenkins, *Baby Mayfield* (Chicago: Moody, 1989), 56.

12. Ibid., 59–60.

Chapter 4: Why Do Women Have Abortions?

1. Madeline Pecora Nugent, "Letter on Abortion of Handicapped Babies," 1990.

2. Larry and Diane Mayfield with Jerry B. Jenkins, *Baby Mayfield* (Chicago: Moody, 1989), 14–15.

Chapter 5: Who Has Been Affected by Abortions?

1. Center for Chronic Disease Prevention and Health Promotion, Pregnancy Epidemiology Br. and Research and Statistics Br., Div. of Reproductive Health, vol. 38, no. 38 (September 29, 1989).

2. David C. Reardon, *Aborted Women Silent No More* (Westchester, Ill.: Crossway, 1987).

3. Anne Speckhard, *The Psycho-Social Aspects of Stress Following Abortion* (Kansas City, Mo.: Sheed & Ward, 1987).

4. *Family Planning Perspectives,* a journal of the Alan Guttmacher Institute, an affiliate of Planned Parenthood (January/February and March/April 1987).

5. Lis Trouten, "Woman Tells of Recovery After Four Abortions," *Twin City Christian* (January 12, 1989).
6. John Stanhope, "How Abortion Affects Men," *Faith Today* (May/June 1988): 26.
7. Ibid., 27.
8. Dr. Phillip Ney, *Child Psychiatry and Human Development*, as quoted in *National Right to Life News* (January 15, 1987): 19.
9. Mary Louise Gans, *National Right to Life News* (January 15, 1987): 19.
10. Gina Kolata, "Fewer Doctors Performing Abortions," *The Los Angeles Daily Journal* (January 16, 1990), as quoted in *Sanctity of Life*, by Charles R. Swindoll (Dallas: Word, 1990), 10–11.
11. Marilyn Derby, "Abortion Takes Its Toll on Nurses, But Most Abortionists Avoid Reality," *National Right to Life News* (January 15, 1987): 22.
12. Ibid.
13. Ibid.

Chapter 6: Physical Effects of Abortion

1. Bernard Nathanson, *Aborting America* (Garden City, N.Y.: Doubleday, 1979), 163.
2. U.S. Department of Health and Human Services, Centers for Disease Control, *Abortion Surveillance Report* (May 1983).
3. C. Everett Koop, *Minneapolis Star and Tribune* (January 1989).
4. T. W. Hilgers and D. O'Hare, "Abortion-Related Maternal Mortality: An In-Depth Analysis," *New Perspectives on Human Abortion* (Frederick, Md.: University Publications of America, 1981), 69.
5. September 21, 1989 ruling of the Circuit Court of Tennessee.
6. U.S. Department of Health and Human Services, Center for Disease Control, 1985.
7. *Dorland's Illustrated Medical Dictionary*, 27th ed. (Philadelphia: W. B. Saunders Co., 1988), 5.
8. F. A. Lyon, "Elective Termination of Pregnancy," *The Bulletin* 33, no. 1 (1989): 45–58.
9. Janice Perrone, *American Medical News* (January 12, 1990): 9, 26–30.
10. A. Rosenfield, "RU-486 and the Politics of Reproduction," *The Female Patient* 14 (1989): 69–74.
11. R. H. Overmyer, "RU-486: Preparing for the Abortion Drug," *Modern Medicine* 58 (February 1990): 50–57.
12. E. E. Balieu, "RU-486 as an Antiprogesterone Steroid," *Journal of the American Medical Association* 262 (1989): 1808–14.
13. S. Ossen and K. Persson, "Post-abortal Pelvic Infection Associated

with Chlamydia Tracomatis and the Influence of Humoral Immunity," *American Journal of Obstetrics and Gynecology* (November 1984): 699–703.

14. R. T. Burkman, "Culture and Treatment Results in Endometritis Following Elective Abortion," *American Journal of Obstetrics and Gynecology* (July 1977): 556–99.

15. Ibid., *Morbidity Risk Among Young Adolescents Undergoing Elective Abortion*, Fertility Control Center, Johns Hopkins Medical Institutions (August 1984): 99–105.

16. "Genital Tract Infection," *OB/GYN News* 20, no. 3 (February 1–14, 1985): 42.

17. Westrom, "Effect of Acute PID on Fertility," *American Journal of Obstetrics and Gynecology* 12, no. 5 (March 1, 1975): 707–13.

18. Adler et al., "Morbidity Associated with PID," *British Journal of V.D.* 58 (1982): 151–57.

19. Westergaard et al., "Significance of Cervical Chlamydia Trachomatis Infection in Post-abortal PID," *OB/GYN* 60, no. 3 (September 1982): 322–25.

20. "Digest: Abortion Fatalities Could Be Prevented by Earlier Diagnosis of Hemorrhage," *Family Planning Perspectives* 16, no. 6 (November/December 1984): 284.

21. K. Dalaker et al., "Delayed Reproductive Complications After Induced Abortions," *Acta Obstet Gynecol Scand* 58 (1979): 491–94.

22. F. A. Lyon, "Elective Termination of Pregnancy," *The Bulletin* 33, no. 1 (1989): 45–58.

23. Tietze, *Induced Abortion: A World Review* (New York: The Population Council, 1983), 83.

24. "Legal Abortion Mortality," *American Journal of Obstetrics and Gynecology* 156, no. 3 (March 1987): 611.

25. Kounitz et al., "Causes of Maternal Mortality in the United States," *Obstetrics and Gynecology* 65 (1985): 605–12.

26. K. Dalaker et al., "Delayed Reproductive Complications After Induced Abortion," *Acta Ostet Gynecol Scand* (1979); and D. Trichoupoulos et al., "Induced Abortion and Secondary Infertility," *British Journal of Obstetrics and Gynecology* 83 (1976): 645–50.

27. A. A. Levin et al., "Ectopic Pregnancy and Prior Induced Abortion," *American Journal of Public Health* 72, no. 3 (March 1982): 253–56; P. Panayotou, "Induced Abortion and Ectopic Pregnancy," *American Journal of Obstetrics and Gynecology* (1972): 507–10; and S. Linn, "The Relationship between Induced Abortion and Outcome of Subsequent Pregnancy," *American Journal of Obstetrics and Gynecology* (May 1983): 136–40.

28. J. M. Barrett et al., "Induced Abortion: A Risk Factor for Placenta Previa," *American Journal of Obstetrics and Gynecology* 141, no. 7 (Dec. 1, 1981): 769–72; and Cotton et al., "The Conservative Aggressive Management of Placenta Previa," *The American Journal of Obstetrics and Gynecology* 137 (1980): 687.

29. Levin et al., "Association of Induced Abortion with Subsequent Pregnancy Loss," *Journal of the American Medical Association* 243 (1980): 2495; Harlap et al., "Prospective Study of Spontaneous Fetal Losses after Induced Abortions," *New England Journal of Medicine* 301, no. 13 (September 27, 1979): 677–81; and *Special Program of Research, Development and Research Training in Human Reproduction: Seventh Annual Report* (Geneva, Switzerland: World Health Organization, 1978).

30. Harlap and Davies, "Late Sequelae of Induced Abortion: Complications and Outcome of Pregnancy and Labor," *American Journal of Epidemiology* 102, no. 3 (1975): 217–24.

31. S. Linn, "The Relationship Between Induced Abortion and Outcome of Subsequent Pregnancy," *American Journal of Obstetrics and Gynecology* (May 1983): 136–140; E. B. Obel, "Pregnancy Complications Following Legally Induced Abortion," *Acta Obstet Gynecol Scand* (1979): 485–90; C. Madore, "A Study on the Effects of Induced Abortions on Subsequent Pregnancy Outcome," *American Journal of Obstetrics and Gynecology* (March 1981): 516–21; J. A. Richardson and G. Dixon, "The Effects of Legal Termination on Subsequent Pregnancies," *British Medical Journal* (1976): 1303–4.

32. S. Linn, "The Relationship Between Induced Abortion and Outcome of Subsequent Pregnancy," *AJOG* (May 1983): 136–140; C. Madore, "A Study on the Effects of Induced Abortions on Subsequent Pregnancy Outcome," *AJOG* (March 1981): 516–21.

Chapter 7: Emotional Effects of Abortion

1. Elisabeth Kubler-Ross, *On Death and Dying* (New York: Macmillan, 1969).

2. Nancy Michels, *Helping Women Recover from Abortion* (Minneapolis: Bethany House, 1988), 90.

3. Vincent Rue, "Abortion in Relationship Context," *International Review of Natural Family Planning* (Summer 1985): 113.

4. Anne Speckhard, *Psycho-Social Stress Following Abortion* (Kansas City, Mo.: Sheed & Ward, 1987), 43.

5. Ibid., 42.

6. Ibid., 42, 45.

7. Linda Riebel and Jane Kaplan, *Someone You Love Is Obsessed with Food* (Center City, Minn.: Hazelden, 1989), 28.

8. Ibid., 29–30.
9. Jeff Van Vonderen, *Good News for the Chemically Dependent* (Nashville: Nelson, 1985), 19.
10. Ibid.
11. Ibid.

Chapter 8: Spiritual Effects of Abortion

1. David Seamands, *Healing for Damaged Emotions* (Wheaton, Ill.: Victor Books, 1985), 15.
2. Ibid., 13.
3. Ibid.
4. Ibid., 14.
5. Anne Speckhard, *Post-Abortion Counseling: A Manual for Christian Counselors* (Falls Church, Va.: Christian Action Council, 1987), 51.
6. Henri J. M. Nouwen. *With Open Hands* (New York: Ballantine, 1972), 26.

Chapter 9: What Is the Conquerors Program?

1. From the *Conquerors Post-Abortion Support Group Leaders Manual*, available for purchase from New Life Family Services.

Chapter 12: Identifying My Feelings

1. *New Webster's Universal Encyclopedia* (New York: Bonanza Books, 1987), 49.
2. Frank Minirth, Paul Meier, and Don Hawkins, *Worry-Free Living* (Nashville: Nelson, 1989), 65.
3. Ibid., 28.
4. Adapted from Frank Minirth and Paul Meier, *Happiness Is a Choice* (Grand Rapids: Baker, 1988), 170–71.
5. Ibid., 171.
6. Ibid.
7. The information from this section is adapted from the *Conquerors Post-Abortion Support Group Leaders Manual*.

Chapter 13: Dealing with My Guilt and Shame

1. Tim Sheehan, *Shame* (Center City, Minn.: Hazelden, 1989), 4–5.
2. John Bradshaw, *Healing the Shame That Binds You* (Deerfield Beach, Fla.: Health Communications, 1988), 89.
3. Jeff Van Vonderen, *Tired of Trying to Measure Up* (Minneapolis: Bethany House, 1989), 23.

Chapter 14: Working Through My Grieving Process

1. Elisabeth Kubler-Ross, *On Death and Dying* (New York: Macmillan, 1969).

2. Anne Speckhard, *Post-Abortion Counseling and Education* (Falls Church, Va.: Christian Action Council, 1987), 43.
3. These suggestions are based on the *Conquerors Post-Abortion Support Group Leaders Manual*, 44–45.

Chapter 15: Taking Responsibility for the Loss of My Child

1. *The New Webster Encyclopedic Dictionary of the English Language* (Chicago: Consolidated Book Publishers), 7.
2. The information from this section is adapted from the *Conquerors Post-Abortion Support Group Leaders Manual.*

Chapter 16: Evaluating My Relationships

1. Tim and Beverly LaHaye, *The Act of Marriage* (Grand Rapids: Zondervan, 1976), 95.
2. Ibid., 124.
3. Ibid., 123.
4. Jeff Van Vonderen, *Tired of Trying to Measure Up* (Minneapolis: Bethany House, 1989), 21.
5. Veronica Ray, *Striking a Balance* (Center City, Minn.: Hazelden, 1989), 7–11.
6. Ibid.

Chapter 18: Improving My Self-Image

1. Josh McDowell, *His Image, My Image* (San Bernadino, Calif.: Here's Life, 1984), 31.

Chapter 19: Continuing My Healing Process

1. *Life Application Bible* (Wheaton, Ill.: Tyndale, 1988), 1818.

Bibliography

Conquerors Post-Abortion Support Group Leaders Manual (Richfield, Minn.: New Life Family Services).

Lynn Heitritter and Jeanette Vought, *Helping Victims of Sexual Abuse* (Minneapolis: Bethany, 1989).

Pam Koerbel, *Abortion's Second Victim* (Wheaton, Ill.: Victor Books, 1986).

Nancy Michels, *Helping Women Recover from Abortion* (Minneapolis: Bethany House Publishers, 1988).

Frank Minirth, Paul Meier, and Don Hawkins, *Worry-Free Living* (Nashville: Nelson, 1989).

Frank Minirth and Paul Meier, *Happiness Is a Choice* (Grand Rapids: Baker, 1988).

John Piper, *Desiring God* (Portland, Ore.: Multnomah, 1986).

David Reardon, *Aborted Women—Silent No More* (Westchester, Ill.: Crossway Books, 1987).

Teri and Paul Reisser, *Help for the Post-Abortion Woman* (Grand Rapids: Zondervan Publishing House, 1989).

Linda Riebel and Jane Kaplan, *Someone You Love Is Obsessed with Food* (Center City, Minn.: Hazelden, 1989).

David Seamands, *Healing for Damaged Emotions* (Wheaton, Ill.: Victor Books, 1985).

Anne Speckhard, *The Psycho-Social Aspects Following Abortion* (Kansas City, Mo.: Sheed & Ward, 1987).

Anne Speckhard, *Post-Abortion Counseling: A Manual for Christian Counselors* (Falls Church, Va.: Christian Action Council, 1987).

Susan M. Stanford, *Will I Cry Tomorrow?* (Old Tappan, N.J.: Revell, 1986).

Jeff Van Vonderen, *Tired of Trying to Measure Up* (Minneapolis: Bethany House, 1989).